"Yolanda Solomon has been a beacon [...]
Her godly insight and reflections are collected here to help us all continue our own transformative journey with Jesus and others."

Lecrae, recording artist and author of *I Am Restored: How I Lost My Religion but Found My Faith*

"As a pastor, I've witnessed firsthand Yolanda Solomon's profound impact as our church's director of discipleship, where she not only teaches with faithfulness to the Word of God but also truly embodies biblical principles. This book seamlessly combines practical advice, rich personal experiences, and robust theological insights, reflecting her years of dedication to discipleship. It's more than just a guide; it's a testament to her deep expertise and passionate commitment to seeing spiritual growth within the body of Christ. This is an indispensable read for anyone looking to enrich their discipleship journey."

Brandon Watts, pastor of Epiphany Church Brooklyn, New York

"Yolanda Solomon disrupts the individualism that has marked discipleship for far too long and restores the communal nature that is embedded in true discipleship—one where we are invited to colabor with God in God's work in the world. This is a must-read for all who are serious about pursuing Christ in authentic ways in today's world!"

Janice McLean-Farrell, Dirck Romeyn Associate Professor of Metro-Urban Ministry at New Brunswick Theological Seminary

"Yolanda Solomon is a chef who has served us a recipe for discipleship that includes all the ingredients of a great meal. In this unique work, she infuses her sage wisdom with biblical exposition and a life well marinated in campus ministry, church leadership, and real-world experiences. Yolanda plates her theologically rich and practical discipleship principles with a delightful blend of relatable stories and culturally relevant anecdotes that offers up a deep dish of fresh and satisfying insights that help us to think deeply and apply broadly what it means to collaborate as sous-chefs with the Master Chef who calls us to 'feed my sheep.'"

Rasool Berry, teaching pastor at the Bridge Church in Brooklyn, New York

DISCIPLESHIP AS HOLY COLLABORATION

HELPING OTHERS FOLLOW JESUS IN REAL LIFE

YOLANDA M. SOLOMON

FOREWORD BY EKEMINI UWAN

An imprint of InterVarsity Press
Downers Grove, Illinois

InterVarsity Press
P.O. Box 1400 | Downers Grove, IL 60515-1426
ivpress.com | email@ivpress.com

InterVarsity Press® is the publishing division of InterVarsity Christian Fellowship/USA®. For more information, visit www.intervarsity.org.

All Scripture quotations, unless otherwise indicated, are taken from The Holy Bible, New International Version®, NIV®. Copyright © 1973, 1978, 1984, 2011 by Biblica, Inc.™ Used by permission of Zondervan. All rights reserved worldwide. www.zondervan.com. The "NIV" and "New International Version" are trademarks registered in the United States Patent and Trademark Office by Biblica, Inc.™

Scripture quotations marked MSG are taken from The Message, copyright © 1993, 2002, 2018 by Eugene H. Peterson. Used by permission of NavPress. All rights reserved. Represented by Tyndale House Publishers.

While any stories in this book are true, some names and identifying information may have been changed to protect the privacy of individuals.

Author photo: Keith Major

The publisher cannot verify the accuracy or functionality of website URLs used in this book beyond the date of publication.

Cover design: David Fassett
Interior design: Jeanna Wiggins
Images: © Pakin Songmor / Moment via Getty Images, © CSA Images via Getty Images,
        © YOTUYA / iStock via Getty Images

ISBN 978-1-5140-0619-1 (print) | ISBN 978-1-5140-0620-7 (digital)

Printed in the United States of America ♾

Library of Congress Cataloging-in-Publication Data
Names: Solomon, Yolanda (Yolanda Michelle), 1978- author. | Uwan, Ekemini,
   writer of foreword.
Title: Discipleship as holy collaboration : helping others follow Jesus in
   real life / Yolanda Solomon ; foreword by Ekemini Uwan.
Description: Downers Grove, IL : InterVarsity Press, [2024] | Includes
   bibliographical references.
Identifiers: LCCN 2023052487 (print) | LCCN 2023052488 (ebook) | ISBN
   9781514006191 (print) | ISBN 9781514006207 (digital)
Subjects: LCSH: Christian life. | African American Christians. | Jesus
   Christ–Example. | BISAC: RELIGION / Christian Ministry / Discipleship |
   RELIGION / Christian Living / Spiritual Growth
Classification: LCC BV4501.3 .S6577 2024 (print) | LCC BV4501.3 (ebook) |
   DDC 248/.5–dc23/eng/20240116
LC record available at https://lccn.loc.gov/2023052487
LC ebook record available at https://lccn.loc.gov/2023052488

30   29   28   27   26   25   24 | 12   11   10   9   8   7   6   5   4   3   2   1

DEDICATION

To Rodney, the love of my life,

and to Samuel and Emmanuel,

my hearts, the love of our lives.

This book is dedicated to every servant of God

trying to hold on to belief and help people believe

at the same time.

CONTENTS

FOREWORD

EKEMINI UWAN

All authority in heaven and on earth has been given to me.
Therefore go and make disciples of all nations, baptizing them
in the name of the Father and of the Son and of the Holy Spirit,
and teaching them to obey everything I have commanded you.
And surely I am with you always, to the very end of the age.

THE LORD JESUS CHRIST, MATTHEW 28:18-20

THESE ARE THE FINAL WORDS OF JESUS, spoken to his disciples before he ascended into heaven, words now known as the Great Commission. The fact that these were the last words Jesus chose to speak to his disciples emphasizes the gravitas of Jesus' commission to his disciples and—by extension—to those of us who are now Jesus' disciples. As we say in the Black church, "I ain't been saved all my life," but I have been walking with the Lord for twenty years now, and what I know to be true is that it takes a village to raise a Christian.

I am the product of such a village. As I sit with the weight of Jesus' powerful and prophetic commission to his disciples and us, I am led to ask the logical and inevitable question: Have we failed to obey the Great Commission?

When I survey the current landscape of the church in the United States across race, class, and denominational lines, pastors and churches are going viral for salaciousness, scandal, cold-heartedness, and all manner of abuse. Then, there are professing Christians who won't put up with sound doctrine, and who balk at Jesus' instruction to deny ourselves, take up our cross, and follow him down the narrow path that leads to life. With sorrow in my heart and tears in my eyes, I have to say that the unfortunate answer to the inevitable question is an emphatic yes: we have failed to obey the Great Commission. Our villages are decimated, and this destruction is not from without but from within.

According to Barna Group, 56 percent of Christians say their faith is private. On the topic of discipleship, only 28 percent of Christians are being discipled, and a measly 5 percent are discipling others. Do you see what I see? The decimation of our villages is an inside job, and it will take an inside job wrought by the power of the Holy Spirit to help the church get back to the kingdom work of obeying the Great Commission. The good news for us is that our God is the God of the comma, not the God of the period. He is not done making the church the beautiful, spotless bride Jesus died to redeem.

For such a time as this, God has raised up one of his very own daughters, Yolanda Michelle Solomon, who has gifted us with this discipleship tome, *Discipleship as Holy Collaboration*. In her literary debut, Yolanda's passion, love, skill, expertise, and heart for discipleship shine brightly over the blighted villages of the American church context. I have had the privilege and honor of not only counting Yolanda as a sister in Christ but also as a friend. For years, I've observed Yolanda's gift for discipleship: her humility, love for people, ability to speak the truth in love, and wise application of the Word of God in the lives of those whom she disciples are a wonder to behold. Yolanda loves discipleship, Yolanda lives discipleship, and Yolanda is the product of villages that have formed her into a disciple and have shaped her view of discipleship. Above all else, her love for Jesus fuels her discipleship posture and praxis, which foregrounds this book.

In March 2021, *Truth's Table,* the podcast I cohost alongside Christina Edmondson, launched our fifth season with a series titled "We Gon' Learn Today," which focused on education in various sectors of society, including the church. When we decided to produce an episode about discipleship, Yolanda was the first person who came to mind for us. Yolanda joined us at the table for the "We Gon' Learn Today: What Is Discipleship?" episode. She blew us away with her candor, wisdom, and knowledge. Our audience of Black women clamored for more of Yolanda's teaching after hearing her on the show, so we invited her to teach the women in our Black Women's Facebook Discipleship group for three weeks. It goes without saying, but as you can imagine, three weeks was not enough to satiate the desire to learn more about being a disciple of Jesus. Still, we were so grateful for her offering to us and our discipleship group.

It's no secret that there is a dearth of discipleship resources written by Black women, which makes this book critically important. Her vantage point as a Black woman who has been discipling people from all walks of life for over ten years makes her uniquely positioned to write a book on discipleship that seamlessly marries the theological with the practical.

Yolanda demystifies discipleship through her exegesis of Scripture and culture, which empowers the reader to disciple others or seek out someone to disciple them.

For years, Yolanda has been reconstructing villages that will raise disciples of Christ who love Jesus, justice, and mercy, who walk humbly with our Thrice Holy God. In *Discipleship as Holy Collaboration*, Yolanda has gifted the church with a clear instruction manual on how to wield the sword of the Spirit with grace and truth in order to do the kingdom work of making disciples. May we all join Yolanda and partner with God in this divine village reconstruction project, which the American church so desperately needs.

1

MY DISCIPLESHIP JOURNEY

In 1999, I spent the spring semester of my junior year of college interning for a TV and film production company and in the post-production office of a TV show that rhymes with "Schmawson's Schmeek." I was so hyped to go to Los Angeles, escape the bootleg Ithaca, New York, "spring" and be back in a real city (like Brooklyn) where I could get my party on for real. My mind danced with thoughts of seasoned food, good weed, and dope parties in real clubs (shoutout to "Club Semesters" in Ithaca for holding me down, but you weren't enough). I was living in Los Angeles for the semester and had big dreams and aspirations, y'all! I was making seventy-five dollars a week, going to industry parties—and after meeting Nice & Smooth at the 1999 Soul Train Music awards you couldn't tell me nothing! I was on track to graduate a semester early with a television and radio production degree and my goals were to network with enough industry big wigs to secure a job offer after graduation.

God changed my plans.

A family friend, who grew up in the same Brooklyn Baptist church that I did, lived and worked in Los Angeles, and I reached out to her as soon as I arrived with hopes that she could connect me with her industry friends. She was a successful film and television actress so I wasn't sure if she would reach back, but she did, and not in the way that I'd hoped.

She reintroduced me to Jesus and saved my life.

Ariyan discipled me without me even knowing it. It started with her offering me rides to get groceries. (I didn't have a car, and I can't think of anything more Christlike than voluntarily driving through LA traffic.) The rides turned into lunches, and the lunches turned into her letting me tag along to industry events where I did my fair share of schmoozing. She was obviously very busy but made time for me. She introduced me to her industry friends and, if I asked, offered up advice about moving through the TV/film industry as a young Black woman. She told me that even though there was fierce competition for acting roles written for Black women, she prayed about the jobs that she would take and trusted God to direct her path. But most importantly, for that entire semester, I watched her sneakily model a Christlike life in front of me. Much of discipleship is caught not taught—and I was watching.

That spring, somehow, I got tickets to the Soul Train Music awards. Lauryn Hill took home four awards, and as we left the Shrine Auditorium the day seemed like it couldn't get any better. But then it did. When I walked into the House of Blues after-party and realized I was in the same room as Busta Rhymes and Whitney Houston, I nearly lost my mind! I set up shop at that open bar and commenced to dranking. Ariyan kept an eye on my underage ratchetry with no judgment. She just hit me with a *lemme me know when you're ready to go* and stayed close while sipping a mocktail and talking to her industry buddies. She always said, "You can be a Christian in this business and still be a Christian in this business." What I caught that night was that it was possible to be a Christian, have biblical convictions, and not be a weirdo. Ariyan had been on full merit scholarship for Alvin Ailey, Harkness Ballet, and Martha Graham but chose to share her gifts and talent as the director of the liturgical dance ministry at her local church. She chose to live as a woman set apart for God's use, even though she had options to do otherwise. She was the same person at the awards show afterparty as she was on car rides to the grocery store. She never switched up. And I was taking it all in.

I also subconsciously compared her to the industry executives that I hoped would offer me a job at the end of my internship. Ariyan had ambition, but, unlike my peers, the industry wasn't everything to her. It was everything to me. I'd be restocking my bosses' mini fridges with Diet Cokes, daydreaming about how to get one of the scripts that I'd written for my screenwriting class into the right hands so I could be set for life. One day I was in the Carsey-Werner intern room watching reruns of *A Different World* when someone ran in and said, "Turn on the news! There's been a shooting at a school!" This was back when school shootings were rare, so everything stopped while we learned about a place called Columbine in Colorado. It got real somber really quick and we interns were sent home early. As I wandered around Studio City that day, I began to think about my life. I remember thinking, *These execs and show writers are everything that I want to be . . . but none of them have joy like Ariyan. Ariyan is the happiest person that I know out here!* Earlier in the semester Ariyan invited me to a worship service at her church, but I didn't go. She offered once or twice again but never pushed it. She just said to me, "If you ever want to come, let me know. Even if you're out and it's late, let me know and come through. I'll leave a spare key in the flowerpot by the front door, and we can go together." After the Columbine shooting, I finally said yes.

Because God has a sense of humor, the Saturday night before I'd planned to visit her church, I went out partying with some friends. We went to a bar and the night ended with my friend being arrested for public drunkenness (apparently that's a crime in Pasadena). While we waited for him to be released, I started to think. It was about an hour drive back to our apartment complex in the valley and as we finally headed home, I began to think about my life again. You get real deep when you're half drunk. I thought about the semester (which was almost over), the relationships and connections I'd made, and what I was going to do with my life. And then—*Oh snap!! Church!!* I thought, *Just go home. You can go another Sunday. It's been a crazy night.* But as we got closer to LA, something shifted, and I told my friends to take me to Ariyan's house. When they dropped me off, I found she'd left a key in the flowerpot by her front door so I could let myself in, just as she'd promised.

When I got in, I marveled at how she'd left Post-its all over the house with instructions on where I could find food, drink, and linens. I remember looking around, whispering a prayer of thanks, and then passing out on the pull-out bed. The next morning, I woke up to Ariyan cooking and playing CeCe Winans, and she was like, "You look awful, we'll go to the second service." And so we headed to church later, and for the first time in a long time, the Word of God penetrated my soul.

The pastor was named Kenneth C. Ulmer, and he preached a sermon called "The Wills on the Wheel" from Jeremiah 18. The premise of the sermon was that God's will was to mold us like a potter shapes clay. In the pastor's analogy, God was the potter (who had a will), we were the clay (who also had a will), and the potter's wheel represented being in the will of God. No matter how marred the clay, or how good or bad it felt to be shaped by God, if the clay stayed on the wheel, it was in "good hands." As he preached, I tried (with my hung-over self) to put myself in the sermon, but the only reference that I had for pottery was the scene from the movie *Ghost* with Demi Moore and Patrick Swayze. Not ideal, I know.

I tried to create a mental picture of what the pastor described and imagined myself as an amorphous, messed-up lump of clay in the corner of a pottery barn with God sitting next to an empty potter's wheel nearby. If I followed the pastor's metaphor, I knew I wasn't on the wheel (or in God's will) and I had no clue how to climb on. I was going to decide what to do with my life after that semester, not God. I was going to decide whether to live in NYC or LA after graduation, not God. I was going to decide what job I took or didn't take, not God. So my question was, *How does a messed-up lump of clay get up on God's pottery wheel—how do I get in God's hands?* And for the first time, without answers, I began to personally wrestle with God's Word for myself. I closed my eyes and began to pray. It's a miracle that I didn't doze off, but in that moment a song came to mind. It was a song that I'd heard many times as a child back in Brooklyn at Mt. Lebanon Baptist Church: "We are climbing Jacob's ladder, we are climbing Jacob's ladder, soldiers of the cross." I began to cry because in that moment, the song seemed cruel. I knew myself, and I knew that in my own strength—even if I white-knuckled it and tried my best to be a "good Christian"—I could never get "high enough" to be in God's will (or on the wheel). That was for Christians like Ariyan.

I wondered about where in the Bible that song came from and, as the sermon continued, I grabbed a pew Bible and searched for Jacob's name. (I knew he was somewhere in Genesis.) Eventually I found the passage where Jacob dreams about a ladder that rests on earth and reaches all the way to heaven. I whispered to myself, "Oh snap. Jesus is the ladder! Jesus is how we get to God!" I probably sounded crazy to the people in my pew, but for the first time in my life, I began to understand why the gospel was good news.

At the close of the sermon, I did a super dramatic gospel stage-play slow walk to the front of the church, and I flung myself on the altar to rededicate my life to Christ. I could barely see through my tears. I flushed all my weed down the toilet, and, by the end of that semester, I was catching multiple buses from the valley to Inglewood for midweek Bible studies. For the first time in my life, Jesus felt like someone I was getting to know personally. Like, I'd always known Jesus, but I had been reintroduced. I even changed my email address to clayinhishands(at)mac.com. As I think about that spring, I'm filled with gratitude toward my parents for taking me to church as a child because a seed was planted within me through those Sunday school Bible stories and old hymns. If you're a parent trying to nudge your children to follow Jesus and feel discouraged because nothing you say seems to be sinking in, be encouraged; God is working.

In the weeks that followed, Ariyan would try her best to answer my questions about applying the Bible to my life. She never made me feel stupid or silly when I pushed back, she just listened . . . a lot. She was firm in her convictions, and she let the Word of God speak for itself—she wasn't really about arguing. Her life was saturated with the gospel even though she wasn't super preachy. She was good news to the people around her. What I mean is that she modeled a life of following in the footsteps of Jesus and had real joy doing it. Even years later I could always call her and ask for advice, prayer, whatever. She would always point me to Jesus and differentiate between her advice and God's Word.

Even though we're on different coasts, we still keep in touch. When I told Ariyan that I was writing about that spring and asked her what she remembered from that time, she said,

> At that time you were a wild chick. But I didn't treat you like a wild chick. Because I didn't have a prescribed three-point discipleship plan. It's not my job to figure out my thing—that's almost cultish—nobody's God but God. My job is to show people how good my God is. I am nothing without God—if I didn't have him where would I be? I'm just a Black girl from Bed-Stuy. God brings people across our path for a reason, and we're responsible for one another. If you cross my path, I should impart goodness to you on your journey. In the industry and in life, people have done me wrong, but I still try to maintain my integrity as a woman of God. Like John the Baptist said, it's not about me. I'm not the one. Jesus is the one! Everybody has their purpose. Once you know what your purpose is you can pour into people. I'm not a reservoir; I'm a river.

EMBODIMENT

Even though I didn't understand it at the time, what made an impression on me is that Ariyan's discipleship was embodied. She didn't just tell me about Jesus, she embodied the generosity of Jesus when she shared her time, talents, friends, advice, and money with me. She told me about Jesus with her life.

John's Gospel describes Jesus' encounter with a powerful Jewish Pharisee named Nicodemus, as well as Jesus' encounter with a Samaritan woman. Jesus treats both Nicodemus and the Samaritan woman as if they are equally worthy of his time and his teaching even though his culture did not. In the same way,

Ariyan embodied the character of Jesus when she didn't change up her personality whether she was talking to me or one of her celebrity friends. She showed me the love of Christ when she would buy me lunch not knowing that my weekly seventy-five-dollar paycheck had run out. She'd joyfully belt out the latest CeCe Winans song in the car whether she was booked or not. I thought I knew everything, and she embodied the patience of Jesus when my belligerent twenty-year-old self tried to give her advice. She listened. She made space for me in her life and even convinced her industry buddies to take me out to lunch and share their advice. She was following Jesus and made space for me to follow alongside her—all while she bore the fruit of the spirit. And she didn't try and disciple me by herself. I remember one Sunday she couldn't drive me to church, so she arranged for a friend to give me a ride. She had community, and she shared it.

One morning Ariyan took me with her to a dance ministry rehearsal that she was leading at church. I think I helped carry her bags and a boombox. Watching her spend her Saturdays empowering scores of people to offer up their bodies as a "living sacrifice" through dance to worship God was powerful, and it made following Jesus seem like something I could do too. Like Jesus, she was "making disciples" by teaching through kinesthetic learning, where palpable touch and movement was part of the lesson about serving others.

It's one thing to use your gifts to serve and love people, it's another thing to include the people that you're mentoring in spaces of ministry so that they can serve beside you. The miracles that Jesus performed on earth functioned as "we do" lessons because the people present didn't only see his miracles and believe—they participated in them. In the Gospel narrative about the wedding in Cana (John 2), Jesus could have turned water in the wine all by himself, but he enlisted the help of the wedding guests and servants. The servants fill the jars to the brim with water, and they also draw it out as wine.

Theologian Richard Bauckham writes that the miracles Jesus performs "are means of seeing the glory of God."[1] In dark times when it's hard for people to see God working, the "we do" lessons we invite mentees into are incredibly formative because they help mentees get a glimpse of God's glory as they experience Christ's body at work in real time. So many people count themselves out of discipleship and spiritual mentoring because of what they don't know; they say: "I don't know enough Bible," "I don't know how to deal with awkwardness," or "I don't like people!"

But following Jesus is about how we embody the love of Jesus (2 Peter 1:5-9, 1 John 3:16) with the new lives Jesus has given us. It's about the outworking of what we believe, motivated by our new God-given affections. So how can we tell the truth about Jesus with our lives? How can we continue Jesus' redemption story with our bodies?

WE FOLLOW JESUS TOGETHER

Christ-centered community is a major key to making disciples because it's a living witness of the gospel that proclaims that the kingdom of God has come on earth. When we make disciples and help people grow in spiritual maturity, we love our neighbor out loud and reflect the abundant generosity of God with our lives. The God of the Bible isn't stingy with who he is. To redeem creation, God revealed himself to his creation through Christ, to give us access to the triune Godhead. The Son reflects the Father's generosity by giving his life away on

---

[1]Richard Bauckham, *Gospel of Glory: Major Themes in Johannine Theology* (Grand Rapids, MI: Baker Academic, 2015), 56.

the cross to save people, and the Father sends the Spirit to reveal God's will to us and progressively transform us to look like Jesus.

When our faith is disembodied and more about mental assent to a set of beliefs and less about presenting our bodies as living sacrifice, it's difficult for people to believe that Jesus is working on earth. If people can't see the arms and legs of "Christ's body" working, how will they believe that the head exists?

Most pastors know that discipleship is God's mechanism for the growth of the body of Christ (Ephesians 4:11-16) and that since Jesus prioritized making disciples in his ministry on earth, then Christ's body should do the same. But the rest of this book isn't about that. It's about the beauty of discipleship. There are many things we know are good and right that we don't do. I know that leafy greens are good for me, but I will choose a Popeyes biscuit over a spinach salad anyway because fat and salt on bread is beautiful. Jesus' discipleship calling is a command that is good and true, and it's also beautiful because following Jesus equals following beauty and truth. When we engage people with the good news of the gospel, we should remember that people are drawn to what is beautiful before they care whether it's true or not. Reason comes in afterward. On this topic, philosopher Blaise Pascal once wrote, "The heart has its reasons which reason knows nothing of. . . . We know the truth not only through our reason but also through our heart."[2] The road to making disciples goes through heart transformation, and we engage people's hearts when we illustrate the sufficiency and beauty of Jesus and the kingdom of God as a beautiful, coherent way of life. Many people are

---

[2]Blaise Pascal, *Pascal's Pensées* (New York: E. P. Dutton & Co., 1958), 77, 80.

hesitant to make disciples because they've fallen out of love with Jesus. In this book I want to engage your heart as we look at Jesus in the Gospels, rediscover His beauty and in doing so reignite a zeal for the beauty of discipleship. In the pages to come, I want to cast a vision for the beauty of Jesus' discipleship calling by exploring how making disciples of Christ is a way to participate (right now) in the abundant life Jesus calls us to.

The Spirit-filled community of the King is the foundation of discipleship. Discipleship is a corporate expression of obedience to God and love for neighbor that allows people to see what Jesus' love looks like in practice. When Christians prioritize discipleship in community, we make Jesus easier to see. The greatest commandment (love God and love people) empowers us to fulfill the Great Commission (make disciples of all nations). In the book of Acts, we see Spirit-filled communities continue the ministry of Jesus as they proclaim the good news of the gospel and embody the love of Jesus. Those communities are an attractive witness of the power and presence of Jesus because their lives make visible "the abundant life" that Jesus promised. Communities have the power to form (or deform) and shape us. The past ten years have shown me the great harm and heart (de)formation that happens when professing Christians fashion Jesus in their own image to gain power and then frame that wanton pursuit of power as discipleship. In this book I will discuss how healthy Spirit-filled Christian communities proclaim the good news of the kingdom by appropriating God's love and grace into the life of the believing community and then bending it out into the world.

I will also put my business in the streets and describe how different faith communities have shaped my own discipleship journey and spiritual formation (for better or for worse). At the core, I will provide practical tools for anyone who wants to take Jesus' discipleship call seriously—whether you're a new Christian, pastor, college campus minister, or lay leader in a local church.

My disciple-making philosophy is simple. Imitate Jesus as you're empowered by the Holy Spirit. Our ability to make disciples is directly related to how we imitate and participate in the divine life that Jesus invites us into. In John 21:1-22, Jesus appears to the very disciples who deserted him to commission them to follow in his footsteps and "make disciples" of all nations. Jesus doesn't ask why they deserted him, and he doesn't scold them. In fact, before Jesus commands Peter to "feed his sheep," he feeds them breakfast.

Jesus knows it's impossible for the "most problematic inhabitants"[3] of creation (a.k.a. humanity) to make disciples of Christ apart from being disciples of Christ. After denying Jesus, Peter had to experience Jesus as a forgiving shepherd before he could shepherd anyone himself. Peter had to experience Jesus as a grace giver before he could testify about the power of God's grace. And the same is true for us. On that beach, Jesus fed his disciples (physically and spiritually) before sending them out to make disciples. In the same way, Jesus empowers us by the Spirit to make disciples because he knows that we can't continue his story in our own strength.

WHAT TO EXPECT

This book is divided into three parts. In part one (chapters two through four), I'll explain how to make disciples by examining Jesus' discipleship strategy as revealed in the New Testament Gospels. Jesus always demonstrates what he asks his disciples

---

[3]Colin Gunton, *Christ and Creation* (Grand Rapids, MI: Eerdmans, 1992), 33.

to do as he empowers us to do it. I'll also take a medium dive into some ugly moments in recent American history to diagnose how idolatry has created a discipleship problem in the United States. But before you get too discouraged, in chapter four, I talk about how Jesus exposes the idolatry in his own cultural context (which is surprisingly similar to ours) and demonstrates a new way of living. In part two (chapters five through eight), I use baking metaphors to describe how to make disciples by following the cruciform recipe of Jesus' life. I also dispel some discipleship myths by exposing the awful evangelism tactics that I used years ago, so that you won't. I'll also talk about how the Christian hip-hop community, a local church Bible study, and how three years of seminary helped me to apply Jesus' discipleship calling to my urban context of NYC. Finally, in part three (chapters nine through twelve), I'll explain practical ways to establish discipleship relationships, structure discipleship meetings, and depend on the Holy Spirit so that you don't burn yourself out.

2

WHAT IS A DISCIPLE?

I GREW UP IN CHURCH. My whole life. Sunshine choir, church punch, junior usher board, youth crusade, Girl Scouts, "The Rapture" movie nights, small groups, "quiet times," alto on the praise team—you get the picture. And over the course of my life in church, I've observed that there are three types of churchgoers.

The first type of Christians are like Black adults who've never learned to play spades. They have a sense that they should have learned the game long ago and desire to learn to play so they can know what's going on at family functions but are too ashamed to ask how to play because they have aged out of the years of respectable teachability. Inside churches across the United States, people feel like they should love God more and enjoy following Jesus but feel like frauds because they don't. Let's call them "hungry but timid." Like Black people who don't know how to play spades, they're too ashamed to ask for help because they've been Christians for "too long" and "should know better." So they sit through church Sunday after Sunday, lacking understanding about how to practically follow Jesus and grow in spiritual maturity. Now, on the same pew (just slide down a lil' bit) are people who desire to be discipled and have taken the risk to ask for spiritual guidance but have been traumatized by other Christians. Existing trauma from past church hurt has left them too fearful of trusting and letting anyone (especially another Christian) into their lives . . . and, like Luther Vandross, they said, "I don't wanna be a fool ever again." They're guarded, attend church anonymously, and "peace out" right after the benediction because trusting someone other than Jesus himself is too risky. At the end of the day, they just want a safe person to learn how to follow Jesus with. They are "wounded sheep."

Finally, sprinkled in these very same churches, are people who try their best to read their Bible, pray, and love their neighbor. They're "busy but bored" believers. They're usually in church leadership, seem to be "plugged in," but feel like something is missing in their spiritual formation. When I talk to "busy but bored" believers and ask if they'd be interested in connecting with and mentoring a "hungry but timid" believer or lovingly coming alongside a "wounded sheep," the response is usually some iteration of "I'm not qualified! I didn't go to seminary, and I don't want to lead someone astray!" or "I don't have the time!" or "I'm an introvert!" Most times, they're the safe person that a "wounded sheep" desires to follow Jesus with, but they've disqualified themselves. Sadly, some become disillusioned with ministry because they've seen discipleship become a means of recruiting people into political culture wars. As disillusionment gives way to unbelief, many end up leaving the church.

All these people are in the same church, maybe in the same pew on any given Sunday, connected by the same Spirit, but separated by fear, trauma, and doubt. My goal in this book is to equip the longtime "busy but bored" believers to be the safe Christ-followers that the "hungry but timid" and "wounded sheep" are praying to find.

Desmond and Carol raised me in Brooklyn, New York. I've attended churches of various sizes in NYC for almost all my life. I've been a member of a Black Baptist church where the Rev. Al Sharpton was the standing Palm Sunday guest preacher, and a member of a predominately White evangelical church, where we gave away water bottles and granola bars with the church address taped on them, as an evangelistic outreach. For the past twenty years, I've taught Bible studies and led discipleship groups in local churches, worked in campus ministry with undergraduate students at Columbia University and Barnard College, and, most recently, I serve as the discipleship director at a Baptist-ish nondenominational church back in Brooklyn.

I've seen pastors and lay church leaders burn themselves out because they try to minister like they're the Holy Spirit incarnate. I've prayed with people who sit in packed-out churches every Sunday hoping to connect with someone but walk out after Communion enveloped in crushing loneliness. I've also known people with incredible pastoral gifts that lay dormant because they believe they're the wrong gender for leadership, or that they need a seminary degree to walk in their God-given calling as a member of the holy priesthood of believers.

A disciple is basically a follower. In the New Testament, we see Jesus Christ call men and women to follow him and promise to transform them. In Matthew 4:19, Jesus proclaims, "Follow me and I'll make you something new" (my paraphrase) and calls what will be the first of many followers to a new and abundant life in him. The Gospel narratives describe how the disciples follow Jesus, learning as they watch him redefine leadership with his life and engage the marginalized as whole people, worthy of love and instruction. Jesus is the just and righteous Davidic king who is literally good news to the poor. He uses his power to bless, not to exploit. Unlike some politicians we know, Jesus is a true public servant. And as his followers experience Jesus bringing restoration, shalom, radical love, and healing wherever he goes, they're transformed by Jesus' embodiment and proclamation of the good news of the kingdom of God. When Jesus touches ritually unclean lepers (Mark 1:41), extends a discipleship call to a tax collector (Mark 2:13-17) and heals a man on the Sabbath (Mark 3:1-6), he uses his power to make room in the kingdom of God for those on the margins of first-century Jewish Palestine.

Jesus teaches that kingdom values are basic: clothe the naked, welcome the stranger, feed the hungry (Matthew 25:31-46). Jesus describes the kingdom of God in many ways but in Mark 10:15 he teaches that his kingdom must be received as a child. On the topic of the kingdom of God, Dr. Clarice J. Martin writes, "The child and slave who are typically relegated to the lowest rung on the patriarchal household ladder become, in the ministry of Jesus, a primary paradigm for authentic discipleship."[1] Jesus calls his disciples to lay down our desire to rule over others, to lay down our desire to live only for ourselves, and to receive new life and follow his example of service born out of love. As Jesus' ministry moves toward Jerusalem, he warns his disciples of his coming crucifixion. One evening over dinner, Jesus cryptically reminds them of this (John 13:36), to which a disciple named Peter responds, "I will lay down my life for you." Jesus tells Peter, "No you won't! Actually, what you WILL do is deny me. Thrice" (my paraphrase). But even still, as the dinner winds down, Jesus

---

[1]Clarice J. Martin, "The Haustafeln (Household Codes) in Afro-American Biblical Interpretation: Free Slaves and Subordinate Women," in *Stony the Road We Trod: African American Biblical Interpretation*, ed. Cain Hope Felder (Minneapolis, MN: Fortress Press, 1991), 211.

calls these disciples friends, and then says, "Greater love has no one than this, to lay down one's life for one's friends" (John 15:13-15). Jesus doesn't call his disciples to lay down their lives for him, instead he calls us to lay down our lives like him.

When I read that Jesus is the Word of God made flesh (John 1:14), it makes me think that Jesus is the extrovert of the Trinity and in his life is everything God wants to say to humanity about how to be human. When Jesus tells his disciples, "I no longer call you servants, because a servant does not know his master's business. Instead, I have called you friends, for everything that I learned from my Father I have made known to you" (John 15:15), Jesus invites his disciples into the divine group chat, to form us to live and love like him so that we might invite others to meet Jesus, who makes the invisible God known. That's discipleship. Good discipleship introduces people to Jesus. Bad discipleship indoctrinates people into cultural idolatry. Making disciples is about introducing people to the friend of sinners, the patient Jesus, the compassionate Jesus, the foot-washing Jesus, the radiance of God's glory Jesus, the listening Jesus, the suffering Jesus, the justice loving Jesus, and the praying Jesus.

JESUS MAKES DISCIPLES

One of the best discipleship models I've ever seen is described in the fourth chapter of the Gospel of John. In this passage Jesus crosses sociocultural boundaries to reveal himself as the incarnate Messiah to a Samaritan woman. As they speak, Jesus has the audacity to engage her like she's a whole human being, to the shock of his male disciples. She recognizes that Jesus is like no other man she's ever met. And she's known a more than a few. She experiences Jesus' humanity and prophetic insight as he asks her for a drink and tells her all about herself.

Because he's God in the flesh, Jesus knows that she's been discarded five times, but Jesus doesn't condemn her.[2] She shares her understanding of who God is with Jesus and, because he's not a stingy Savior, Jesus reveals his messianic secret to her, and a disciple is made. But that's just the beginning.

We make disciples after we encounter the truth, are transformed by the truth, and, in love, invite others to meet the truth that has changed us. The Samaritan woman's encounter with Jesus is so transformative that she sprints off in the direction of the same community that did her dirty to introduce anyone who will listen to this Messiah who is both love and truth. After the Samaritan woman understands that Jesus is the Messiah, she leaves her water can behind at the well because her soul thirst has been quenched. And it doesn't end there. Her testimony about Jesus causes other Samaritans to want to encounter the truth, love, and beauty of Jesus for themselves (John 4:30, 39). After she runs off and his disciples try and convince Jesus to eat, he says, "My food is to do the will of him who sent me and to finish his work" (John 4:34). As with the Samaritan woman, Jesus calls modern-day disciples to be enlivened by continuing the work of God as we introduce people to Jesus and his kingdom so that they can experience love and truth for themselves.

In one of my favorite Gospel narratives, Jesus pulls up to Lake Gennesaret where a group of men are fishing. Jesus asks one of them, Simon Peter, to use his boat so he can be seen by the crowds while he teaches. After Jesus finishes teaching, he

---

[2]The Samaritan woman was discarded because only men were allowed to issue a certificate of divorce (Deut 24:1). Jesus never rebukes the Samaritan women for "living in sin." Reading moral failure into the character of the Samaritan woman flows from a hermeneutic that sees the only goal of the gospel as deliverance from individual sins as opposed to also being about deliverance from sinful systems of oppression.

asks Peter to participate in a miracle, which leads Peter to a shame-filled confession of sin. Jesus responds to Peter's shame by calling Peter to himself for the purpose of transformation, and a disciple is made. Throughout Scripture we see this pattern of people being changed by Jesus' presence and proclamation, following Jesus, being empowered by Jesus to minister alongside him, and then being sent out to minister, empowered by the Holy Spirit. My friend Lourdes, who is an educator, explained Jesus' disciple-making strategy to me like this: "Jesus' didactic was grounded in the pedagogical structure of 'I do, we do, you do' which is a direct model, gradual-release guided practice, and independent practice." So Jesus' discipleship strategy looks like this:

1. People encounter Jesus and his redemptive power and love, and he calls them to follow him.

2. Jesus creates space for his followers to observe him through many "I do" lessons (Mark 9:15-29).

3. Jesus conducts "we do" lessons as he ministers to people alongside his disciples (Matthew 14:13-20).

4. Jesus sends his disciples out in groups for "you do" ministry with instructions while Jesus hangs back (Luke 10:1-20).

On many occasions, the "we do" and "you do" lessons don't go well because Jesus' disciples are incredibly flawed (just like you and me). But what's wild to me is Jesus' bold promise that this flawed group of followers will continue his mission after his ascension by doing "even greater things" than he has (John 14:12), empowered by the Holy Spirit. Before his ascension Jesus commands his followers to "go and make disciples of all nations, baptizing them in the name of the Father and Son and of the Holy Spirit, and teaching them to obey everything I have commanded you. And surely I am with you always, to the very end of the age" (Matthew 28:19-20)

As a new Christian in my early twenties, I remember reading Matthew 28:19-20 and wondering, *How can I make disciples? I'm a mess. How can I do something that it seems like only God can do? How will Jesus "be with me"?* Over time, I realized that Jesus' discipleship calling is the fulfillment of God's original calling for humanity to be fruitful and multiply. Biologically we all can't give birth, but every Christ-follower is called to be a spiritual midwife as the Holy Spirit births "children born not of natural descent, nor of human decision or a husband's will, but born of God." (John 1:13) In the same way the first humans couldn't fulfill the creation mandate to "be fruitful and multiply" without each other, we can't make disciples apart from the community of redeemed servants that we've been saved into.

Discipleship is a miraculous group project that Jesus invites people into. It's a holy collaboration. In John 10:27, Jesus says, "My sheep listen to my voice, I know them, and they follow me." The plural pronouns in this passage reveal that the context of this parable is a pen of sheep. When God is speaking but the trials of life make it hard for me to hear God's voice, I can get the "CliffsNotes" from a brother or sister in Christ because the Shepherd speaks to them too. We can't follow Jesus alone. To make disciples of Christ, you must be a disciple of Christ, connected to the body of Christ.

In the Old Testament, God commands people to use their gifts to beautify the tabernacle where God meets with the Israelites and mediates his blessings (see Exodus 35:4–36:7). In the same way, when we make disciples, we use our gifts to invite people into the body of Christ so that Jesus can sanctify and beautify his new temple (the church) from the inside out with compassion, humility, forgiveness, patience, and love (Colossians 3:12-14). We grow in spiritual maturity as we use our spiritual gifts to creatively participate in the holy work of making disciples and teaching people how to grow in spiritual maturity, empowered by the Spirit.

The beauty of discipleship is that Jesus enables what he commands by ensuring that the same Spirit that empowered him for ministry (Luke 4:14) is given to his followers (Luke 24:48-49) to empower us to make disciples. In his book *Community of the King*, Howard A. Snyder writes, "To say the church is the agent of God's mission on earth is equivalent to saying the church is the agent of the kingdom of God."[3]

Individually, disciples are God's handiwork, and corporately, disciples are the body of Christ. The greater our understanding of ourselves and the church as the work of God animated by the Spirit, the easier it will be for the church to do the work of God in making disciples of Christ and living as agents of the kingdom of God on earth.[4] Church communities are a vital part of making disciples because Christ and the church are a unified, interdependent living organism (see Ephesians 1:22-23). The fruit we bear is proof that we're alive in Christ, united with Christ, and united to one another (Philippians 1:9-11; 2 Corinthians 5:17).

Because Jesus' earthly ministry has ended and his present ministry operates in us through the Holy Spirit, good discipleship must introduce people to Christ's body or else the promise of the abundant life is too theoretical. Jesus taught his disciples that bearing fruit is evidence that this entire "being

---

[3]Howard A. Snyder, *The Community of the King* (Downers Grove, IL: InterVarsity Press, 2004), 13.
[4]Snyder, *Community of the King*, 14.

born again" thing is real (John 15:8) and that following Jesus isn't only about what we believe, it's also about the outworking of that belief. When people see a tangible witness of the love of Jesus in real time, it glorifies God and energizes our faith in God. If we try to make disciples apart from the indwelling Spirit we won't bear fruit (John 15:4), and if we try to "go it alone" and make disciples disconnected from the body of Christ, we'll burn out.

What we know as the four Gospels (Matthew, Mark, Luke, and John) are introductions to life of Jesus. Disciple-making is what happens when Spirit-led people colabor with God (1 Corinthians 3:5-9) and continue to introduce people to Jesus as the Spirit transforms and teaches everyone involved (1 Corinthians 2:12-13). Making disciples is about introducing people to "the truth," not our truth, and helping them to grow in spiritual maturity as we teach them how to seek God and hear from God through spiritual disciplines. This can be tricky because objectivity is a myth. We all read Scripture through our cultural, gendered, and socioeconomic lenses, and, if we're not careful, and we can teach people that our cultural preferences are God's will. But friends share. And Jesus calls his disciples his friends. Jesus promises to share the Holy Spirit to help us discern where the voice of Jesus ends, and our cultural bias begins. Making disciples requires a holy imagination and lots of faith (Mark 11:22-24), but united with Christ—the cornerstone who gives stability to the household of faith—we can introduce people to Jesus and invite them to follow him.

3

DIAGNOSING THE
DISCIPLESHIP PROBLEM

ONE OF THE CLEAREST COMMANDS Jesus gives is, "follow me." However, what it means to follow Jesus means so many different things to American Christians these days. The simultaneous pandemics of systemic racism, Covid-19, and the 2016 presidential election have had an outsized effect on discipleship in local churches across the United States and have contributed to chasmic theological and ideological polarization of Christians in the United States.[1] As of this writing, there are multiple best-selling books on Amazon promoting Christian nationalism. I didn't even know Amazon had a *nationalism* book category! Recently, the president of a large American seminary preached that Christians "are unfaithful" as Christians if they "vote wrongly."[2] One year after the murder of George Floyd led to

---

[1] The most substantial cultural and political divides in the United States are between White Christians and Christians of color.

[2] "We have a responsibility to make certain that Christians understand the stewardship of the vote, which means the discipleship of the vote, which means the urgency of the vote, the treasure of the vote . . . and they need to understand that insofar as they do not vote, or they vote wrongly, they are unfaithful because the vote is a powerful stewardship." Albert Mohler, "Pray Vote Stand Summit 2022," First Baptist Church of Atlanta, September 14, 2022, www.youtube.com/watch?v=9WlsGkB8Fzw.

unprecedented global protests, a 2021 national poll showed that some Christians believed that systemic racism is embedded in American society and institutions and are motivated to address racial injustice, while other Christians think racism isn't really a big deal—much less a "gospel issue."[3] According to a 2018 *New York Times* article, this difference in beliefs is causing a "quiet exodus" of Black Christians from multiethnic churches.[4] How can we introduce people to Jesus and make disciples if Christians disagree on who Jesus is or on what matters to Jesus? Jesus taught that a divided household will crumble (Matthew 12:25) and I'm not sure if the household of faith is crumbling, but people are leaving the house. Research conducted by the Cooperative Election Study recently revealed that politics have had a huge impact in the pews.[5] Regarding this research, political scientist, author, and pastor Ryan Burge wrote, "In between 2016–2022, Democratic Gen-Xers and older millennials were the largest demographic to stop attending church, while their Republican generational counterparts' attendance remained the same. The same research revealed that 54% of Gen Z Democrats

---

[3]Barna's "Beyond Diversity" report concluded, "Only two in five white practicing Christians (38%) believe the U.S. has a race problem. This percentage more than doubles, however, among Black practicing Christians (78%). . . . Data show that three in five white practicing Christians (61%) take an individualized approach to matters of race, saying these issues largely stem from one's own beliefs and prejudices causing them to treat people of other races poorly. Meanwhile, two-thirds of Black practicing Christians (66%) agree that racial discrimination is historically built into our society and institutions. . . . Seven in 10 Black practicing Christians (70%) report being motivated to address racial injustice. Only about one-third of white practicing Christians (35%) says the same." Barna, "Black Practicing Christians Are Twice as Likely as Their White Peers to See a Race Problem," June 17, 2020, www.barna.com/research/problems-solutions-racism.
[4]Campbell Robertson, "A Quiet Exodus: Why Black Worshipers Are Leaving White Evangelical Churches," *New York Times*, September 3, 2018, www.nytimes.com/2018/03/09/us/blacks-evangelical-churches.html.
[5]Brian Schaffner, Stephen Ansolabehere, and Marissa Shih, "Cooperative Election Study Common Content, 2022," Harvard Dataverse, 2023, V2, https://doi.org/10.7910/DVN/PR4L8P.

are now atheist, agnostic or nothing compared to 28% of Republicans during that 8-year span."[6] According to a national Pew study, people who identify as Christian have decreased from 90 percent of the US population in 1972 to 64 percent in 2020.[7]

As I serve in my local church leadership, I've also seen firsthand how the simultaneous pandemics of Covid-19, systemic racism and social unrest have exacerbated the pandemic of loneliness in churches, which existed well before March 2020. According to the *New York Times*, one million people live alone in NYC. "In a recent citywide survey by the New York Health department, 57% of people said they felt lonely some or most of the time, and two-thirds said they felt socially isolated in the prior month. An often-cited meta-analysis by Julianne Holt-Lunstad of Brigham Young University compared the risk effects of loneliness, isolation and weak social networks to smoking 15 cigarettes a day."[8]

So, social isolation is as bad for our health as chain smoking, but for many it's preferable to the idolatry and lovelessness that they see permeating pulpits and pews across the United States. For many people, loneliness is preferable to church hurt. In a December 2022 poll of people who once identified as Christian but no longer do, what respondents missed the most was community, and by an overwhelming amount.[9]

---

[6]"Did the Election of Donald Trump Drive People from the Pews? The Impact of MAGA on Young Gen X/Older Millennial Democrats," Ryan Burge, *Graphs about Religion* (blog), April 30, 2023, www.graphsaboutreligion.com/p/did-the-election -of-donald-trump.

[7]Pew Research Center, "Modeling the Future of Religion in America," September 13, 2022, www.pewresearch.org/religion/2022/09/13/modeling-the-future-of -religion-in-america.

[8]John Leland, "How Loneliness is Damaging Our Health," *New York Times*, April 20, 2022, www.nytimes.com/2022/04/20/nyregion/loneliness-epidemic.html.

[9]Brandon Flannery, "I Asked People Why They're Leaving Christianity, and Here's What I Heard," Baptist News Global, December 13, 2022, https://baptistnews.com /article/i-asked-people-why-theyre-leaving-christianity-and-heres-what-i-heard.

What I see from my church pew in NYC is that even though the statistics show that people are starved for community, they hesitate to seek it out in local churches because spiritual abuse, White Christian nationalism, prosperity preaching, and political idolatry have replaced Jesus Christ as the chief cornerstone in many churches across the United States.[10]

A vital part of my job involves phone calls with new visitors to our church. I ask about where they are in their faith journey to suggest various contexts for virtual, one-on-one, and peer discipleship. I've had countless conversations with people whose initial visit to our church was the first time they'd stepped foot in a church in years. Many shared that they preferred to stream worship services at home for fear of coming back to church and being re-exposed to and retraumatized by racism, misogynoir, or spiritual abuse from Christians. One young woman began our conversation by asking me point blank, "What part of myself do I have to leave at the door in order to be a Christian?" On another call, an Asian American woman shared with me that she'd left a church she'd been a part of for many years when she began to see "red flags around race, class, and gender" and had to leave. She told me that even though she'd led Bible studies and helped with the counseling ministry, she had to leave that church for the sake of her mental health. Another person who joined my discipleship class had been a part of two different churches where the lead pastors were spiritually (and sexually) abusive to congregants. They told me they feared the issue wasn't morally depraved pastors alone, but the hierarchical structure of churches that are set up to produce narcissistic and abusive leadership. An

---

[10]Tess Owen, "Christian Nationalism Drove These People Out of Their Churches," *Vice News*, July 18, 2022, www.vice.com/en/article/v7vew9/christian-nationalism -churches.

African American woman told me that her former pastor told a relative of hers that they should leave if the church wasn't "woke enough" for them. And finally, a young man who'd been in leadership at a local megachurch said, "I left before the documentary about the scandal came out." These folks and others like them are "Christian refugees" who've left churches but are taking the risk to come back—with trepidation—hoping to find a safe household of faith.

In the Gospels, Jesus teaches his disciples that sacrificial love is how people will know that they're really his disciples (John 13:34) and that loving God and loving their neighbor as themselves is the greatest commandment (Matthew 22:37-39). We follow Jesus as disciples by living a laid-down life of love (John 15:13) empowered by the hype man of the Trinity, the indwelling Holy Spirit (John 14:26). According to Jesus, if you understand and do these things, "You're not far from the kingdom of God" (Mark 12:34). Conversely, idolatry and lovelessness are the kryptonite to Jesus' discipleship calling because, in the words of Bethany Hanke Hoang, "Failing to love God leads to idolatry while failing to love others leads to injustice."[11]

We're wired to worship. Like water, our worship has to go somewhere. If we don't obey Jesus' call to love the Lord our God and our neighbor as ourselves (plot twist—everyone is our neighbor), we *will* love something else and trust and obey (worship) that thing to "save us" from whatever we fear. As James K. A. Smith writes in his book *You Are What You Love*, "Worship is at the heart of discipleship."[12] What we worship affects how we love and live.

---

[11]Bethany Hanke Hoang and Kristen Deede Johnson, *The Justice Calling: Where Passion Meets Perseverance* (Grand Rapids, MI: Brazos Press, 2016), 17.

[12]James K. A. Smith, *You Are What You Love: The Spiritual Power of Habit* (Grand Rapids, MI: Brazos Press, 2016), 25.

This means that anything that involves worship can disciple people, for good or for bad. Smith explains the power of habit to shape who, what, and how we love, and what that means for discipleship. He writes, "Because love is a habit, our hearts are calibrated through imitating exemplars and being immersed in practices that, over time, index our hearts to a certain end. We learn to love then, not primarily by acquiring information about what we should love, but rather through practices that form the habits of how we love."[13]

This explains how scrolling on Instagram every day can form what we love (about ourselves and others) much more powerfully than going to church can form what we love. This explains how watching the New York Knicks play basketball for over thirty-five years has formed my heart to love them even though they break my heart every season. This explains how millions of self-proclaimed Christians can be discipled by cable news into fear and idolatry instead of the teachings and life of Jesus Christ. Following Smith's logic, because we are wired to worship, our habits shape what we love (or don't love). We learn to love God and people through practices that form how we love God and people. This means discipleship is more about being formed by the Spirit of Christ as we worship than by an endless pursuit of memorizing doctrine and information about Jesus.

Jesus had habits. And they revealed how he loved. Or did Jesus' habits shape how he loved? Maybe it was both. For instance, Jesus had a habit of intimate table fellowship with strangers. Reading through the Gospels, it seems like everyone Jesus met was already a friend. The Gospel of Matthew recounts Jesus telling his disciples, "'I was a stranger and you

---

[13]Smith, *You Are What You Love*, 21.

invited me in.' . . . Then the righteous will answer him, . . . 'When did we see you a stranger and invite you in?' . . . The King will reply, 'Truly I tell you, whatever you did for one of the least of these brothers and sisters of mine, you did for me'" (Matthew 25:35-40). As an exile from glory, Jesus identifies with the lowly (the stranger, the prisoner, the hungry, the sick) and in a culture where "stranger" was synonymous with enemy, he teaches his disciples that the kingdom of God is a place where strangers are welcomed. When Jesus teaches that he's "the good shepherd" who "lays down his life for the sheep," the metaphor implies that he will give his life for all people. "I have other sheep that are not of this sheep pen. I must bring them also. They too will listen to my voice, and there shall be one flock and one shepherd." (John 10:14-16). Sheep are a metaphor for people, and Jesus practices what he preaches by embodying the good news of the kingdom by extending his love to people of all ethnicities (Luke 17:12-19).

In her book *Holy Imagination*, Rev. Dr. Judy Fentress-Williams writes about why Samaritans were the cultural enemies of Jewish people in Jesus' day and how "The level of hostility between Jews and Samaritans was high, as each group claimed to be the legitimate heirs of Abraham."[14] On a walk to Jerusalem, Jesus' disciples get into a skirmish with some Samaritans who don't welcome Jesus (Luke 9:51-56). The disciples ask Jesus if they should "call fire down" on the Samaritans, and Jesus rebukes them. This passage reveals how people can walk with Jesus and impose their cultural biases on him. Jesus' rebuke communicates that then and now he doesn't need his disciples to defend him from who we perceive Jesus' cultural enemies to

---

[14]Judy Fentress-Williams, *Holy Imagination: A Literary and Theological Introductions to the Whole Bible* (Nashville: Abingdon Press, 2021), 237.

be. Culture wars are not Christian discipleship. There's no "us" and "them" in the kingdom of God. If we do have enemies as disciples of Christ, we're called to love them (Matthew 5:44).

In the New Testament, the word translated "stranger" (*xenos*) is the Greek root of the word *xenophobia*, which is defined by *Merriam-Webster* as "fear and hatred of strangers or foreigners." Despite the pervasive teaching in the New Testament that God is uniting Jew and Gentile in Christ and calling disciples to "show hospitality to strangers" (Hebrews 13:1-2), many Christians do not. How can this be? Well, habits are powerful things. Christians who habitually watch media that reports that violent immigrants are taking over the United States with the goal of destroying and replacing them are being discipled by cable news.[15] The act of watching television is forming who, what, and how they love (or don't love). For example, according to the Public Religion Research Institute (PRRI), "Two-thirds (66%) of white evangelical Protestants say that immigrants are invading the United States, the only religious group with majority agreement on the question. . . . Among religious groups, white evangelicals stand out in their perceptions of newcomers to the country as a threat: Two-thirds (67%) of white evangelical Protestants say newcomers are a threat to American traditions."[16] Sunday only comes once a week and alas, xenophobic propaganda is available 24/7. Xenophobia is the antithesis of Jesus' character. And so, the "cultural liturgy"[17] of habitually imbibing cable news that dehumanizes

---

[15]Tucker Carlson, "Tucker Carlson: The Great Replacement Is an Electoral Strategy," Fox News, July 19, 2022, www.foxnews.com/opinion/tucker-carlson-great-replacement-electoral-strategy.

[16]PRRI Staff, "A Nation of Immigrants? Diverging Perceptions of Immigrants Increasingly Marking Partisan Divides," PRRI, March 12, 2020, www.prri.org/research/a-nation-of-immigrants-diverging-perceptions-of-immigrants-increasingly-marking-partisan-divides.

[17]Smith, *You Are What You Love*, 22, 29.

immigrants, coupled with an "America is Lord" mentality, is how Christians can be discipled into xenophobia, and make disciples by introducing people to a xenophobic version of Jesus, despite the witness of Scripture calling God's people to love the foreigner. We have a discipleship problem.

DISCIPLESHIP, POWER, AND IDOLATRY

On January 6, 2021, I was fasting. Fasting is my least favorite spiritual discipline (I like my food and drink), but every January my church corporately fasts from food and media in order to encourage collective prayer without the noise of media consumption. By day three of the fast, I'd stopped missing food, but I deeply missed arguing with people on Twitter. That day, my phone rang in the afternoon; when I picked up, my father asked me, "Are you watching the news?" I said, "No. I'm fasting from television this week." He said, "I think you should turn on the news." When I turned on the television in my children's room, I wasn't prepared for what I saw. People draped in flags that read "Jesus Is My Savior; Trump Is My President" breaking windows at the US Capitol. A man holding a flag in one hand with an image of former president Trump shooting an automatic rifle, and with a flag in his other hand that read "Make America Godly Again." I sat down on the floor. I turned to another news station in time to see live footage of a woman singing "Peace in the name of Jesus" near a noose hanging from makeshift gallows on the US Capitol building lawn while a mob climbed through broken windows and doors to stop the joint session of the US Congress from certifying the results of the 2020 presidential election. One sign simply read, "Jesus. Guns. Trump." I said to myself, "This is a revival meeting. This is church."

It was embodied worship. The Scriptures give a prognosis of untreated idolatry: "Those who make them [idols] will become like them, and so will all who trust in them" (Psalm 115:8; 135:18). If our idol is money, then discipleship is about growing your bank account by any means necessary. If our idol is personal freedom, then discipleship is protesting for the right to disengage from public health practices (in the name of religious freedom) that protect vulnerable segments of the population. If our idol is a nation, we grow in spiritual maturity and serve that idol by serving, worshiping, and defending our nation. Let's stay here for a minute.

Nations and political ideologies make for fickle gods because they need defending. Idolatry disguised as nationalism can lead to making our enemies God's enemies, and then waging war "on God's behalf." If Christians conflate building the kingdom of God with gaining political power and Christians *lose* political power, then to those Christians, the kingdom of God is in trouble. By this logic, discipleship looks like marching around the US Capitol blowing a shofar to protest the results of a fair and free election.[18] Those who make an idol of America (or any nation) believe that *God* is in danger if their vision of *America* is threatened by whatever they fear. In Psalm 115:4-8, the psalmist explains that idolatry can make people act in very inhumane ways because worship is formative.

In the days that followed January 6, 2021, the images and video I saw on the local news rendered me speechless, but I was most struck by the prayers I heard. Once the insurrectionists breached the US Senate chamber, they prayed for God's favor: "Thank you, divine, omniscient, omnipotent, and omnipresent Creator God, for blessing each and every one of us here and

---

[18]Alyssa Wilkinson, "Why Pro-Trump Evangelicals Brought Shofars to DC This Week," Vox, January 8, 2021, www.vox.com/2021/1/8/22219595/shofar-evangelical-trump-jericho-march-judaism.

now. Thank you divine Creator God for surrounding and filling us with the divine omnipresent white light of love and protection, peace and harmony. Thank you for allowing the United States of America to be reborn. Thank you for allowing us to get rid of the communists, the globalists, and the traitors within our government. We love you and we thank you. In Christ's holy name we pray! Amen."[19] We have a discipleship problem.

On May 14, 2022, a man walked into a Tops Supermarket in Buffalo, New York, and shot thirteen people, ten of whom died. Law enforcement later found a 180-page document written by the murderer, which stated the "U.S. should belong only to white people. All others, the document said, were 'replacers' who should be eliminated by force or terror. The attack was intended to intimidate all non-white, non-Christian people and get them to leave the country."[20] Who discipled that man? Who and what is discipling you? As I continued to read about this tragedy, I discovered that the murderer was not a professing Christian but had been discipled by the white supremacist "replacement theory" and as a result took the lives of ten Black people who had the misfortune of going grocery shopping that day. As I lamented, I recalled a similar tragedy in 2015 involving a man who was a baptized member in good standing at St. Paul's Lutheran Church in Columbia, South Carolina, when he murdered nine Black men and women during a Bible study at Emanuel AME Church in Charleston, South Carolina.[21] In his

---

[19]*New Yorker*, "A Reporter's Footage from Inside the Capitol Siege," YouTube, January 17, 2021, https://youtu.be/270F8s5TEKY?t=475, at 8:00.

[20]Deepti Hajela, Aaron Morrison, and Brendan Farrington, "Buffalo Shooting Latest Example of Targeted Racial Violence," Associated Press, May 16, 2022, https://apnews.com/article/buffalo-shooting-targeted-racial-violence-ad45b4c56e74a4ec606c0a7e44694a19.

[21]Robert P. Jones, "Saving Our Churches from Dylann Roof's White Jesus," Baptist News Global, October 4, 2021, https://baptistnews.com/article/saving-our-churches-from-dylann-roofs-white-jesus.

prison manifesto, the man wrote, "Christianity doesn't have to be this weak, feeble, cowardly religion. There is plenty of evidence to indicate that Christianity can be a warrior's religion."[22] The discipleship problem in the United States is a matter of life and death. In the words of Ekemini Uwan, "Disentangling white supremacy from the faith should be an essential part of discipleship"[23] because culture wars are literally killing people.

SEEK THE KINGDOM OF WHO?

So what matters to Jesus? To make disciples of Christ, we must know. Let's start at the beginning. Genesis 1 describes how Elohim (God) creates a kingdom and commands life by his word. In her groundbreaking book *The Very Good Gospel*, author and activist Lisa Sharon Harper writes extensively about the role that power plays in the creation narratives. Harper explains how God uses his power to provide an opulent world for his creation. In love God "shares power" with the human by commanding him to serve and protect creation.[24] But according to Genesis 2:18, it's not "good" for only one human to share power with God. So, God creates a "helper that corresponds to" the human to be a necessary ally in reflecting God's image and in ruling over creation. God mandates that dominion (power) will be a shared human responsibility, and when the man sees the woman, he bursts into song because God has supplied what he lacked. There is abundant provision, diversity, complementarity, and unity. There is no scarcity. There is nothing for humanity to fear.

---

[22]USA v Roof, "Government Exhibit 500," January 5, 2017, www.uscourts.gov/courts/scd/cases/2-15-472/exhibits/GX500.pdf.

[23]Ekemini Uwan, Christina Edmondson, and Michelle Higgins, *Truth's Table: Black Women's Musings on Life, Love, and Liberation* (New York: Convergent Books, 2022), 65.

[24]Lisa Sharon Harper, *The Very Good Gospel: How Everything Wrong Can Be Made Right* (Colorado Springs, CO: WaterBrook Press, 2016), 41, 42.

However, there's another voice in the garden with another story about God. The story goes something like this, "God is stingy! God can't be trusted! God is using his power to keep knowledge from y'all!!" And just like that, fear that God is withholding knowledge leads humanity to put their trust in knowledge instead of God to save them. It leads humanity to reject God's invitation to partner with him to rule over creation. Harper explains that Genesis 3 describes how "very good" tragically goes to "very bad" when humanity believed a "story that led to distrust of God, which led (the) humans to choose their own way to peace, fulfillment, and wholeness."[25]

Because of sin, humans that were originally created to rule over creation began to rule over one another (Genesis 3:16). Lack of trust in God's provision and character led them to make an idol of what they believed was being kept from them. Whether in the Garden of Eden, or on the steps of the US Capitol, a distorted view of God's character leads to idolatry. Idolatry pushes God off his throne and motivates us to climb on and take matters into our own hands (Ezekiel 8:12; Matthew 26:51-21). Idolatry happens when our fears nudge us to trust in (worship) something other than God to save us from what we fear. Idolatry skews our view of what people, places, and things are for and causes us to place redemptive weight on things that can't bear it. But fear isn't the problem. We all have fears because we're human. But what do we do with our fears? Do we let our fears drive us away from or toward God? Toni Braxton has a song called "Love Should Have Brought You Home." Ideally our fears should "bring us home" to God to gain wisdom and clarity.

---

[25]Harper, *The Very Good Gospel*, 48.

What story do you believe about God's character and provision today? Does that story drive you to trust God more or less? Who gets to decide who God's enemies are? What story is your faith community telling you about what matters to God, who God loves, and what God desires? The answers to these questions inform how we make disciples, but the good news is that God isn't stingy with wisdom (James 1:5). Let's look to Jesus.

4

A NEW KIN·DOM

THE CREATION NARRATIVE IN GENESIS 3 reveals how a distorted view of God leads to a distorted view of what it means to worship God. If Jesus came to make God known and proclaim that the kingdom of God had come to earth through him, then misunderstanding Jesus' character and the culture of the kingdom of God is a key to understanding our modern-day discipleship problem. When we use religion as a tool to gain power (political or otherwise) and shame and exclude our cultural enemies, discipleship becomes a means of recruiting foot soldiers in our culture wars, not a way to populate the countercultural kingdom of God. In Acts 1:6-8, Jesus tells the apostles that the kingdom of God isn't about empire building and that the prophetic promises about the restoration of Israel will be fulfilled in a way transcends Jerusalem's borders.

Jesus tells his disciples that they will be filled with the Holy Spirit (Isaiah 32:15) to be Jesus' witnesses (Isaiah 43:12) to all peoples and nations (Isaiah 49:5-6). Their discipleship will be influenced and empowered by the Holy Spirit, who will keep them from idolatry and guide them into truth (Isaiah 30:21-22). They will be witnesses to all kinds of people, even "to the ends of the earth." The first-century community of Christ-followers was great at making disciples—Luke records that "the Lord added to their number daily those who were being saved" (Acts 2:47). So how'd they do it?

Empowered by the Spirit, they followed in Jesus' footsteps and used their apostolic authority to preach the gospel and be agents of healing, even when it threatened the status quo (see Acts 4:2-10). As disciples and disciple-makers we have much to learn from how Jesus exposes and rejects the idols in his cultural context, calls us to follow in his footsteps, and invites us to participate in populating the kingdom of God his way.

In the past, when thinking about the (dis)unity of the American church and how idolatry has permeated it, I used to say, "Jesus is the head of the church, not money or political ideology! If the church could just come under the lordship of Christ and submit to Jesus' law of love then we could focus on making disciples of Christ." But Jesus isn't incarnated as a politician who passes legislation to outlaw idolatry; instead, he embodies a countercultural way of living, rooted in love, to orient people's hearts toward living as image bearers of God. Let's look at one example in the Gospel of Matthew.

> The devil took him to a very high mountain and showed him all the kingdoms of the world and their splendor. "All this I will give you," he said, "if you will bow down and worship me."
>
> Jesus said to him, "Away from me, Satan! For it is written: 'Worship the Lord your God, and serve him only.'" (Matthew 4:8-10)

When tempted to idolatry, Jesus responds by quoting the Law that YHWH gave the people of Israel during their wilderness journey. The irony of Jesus quoting Deuteronomy 6:13 in response to Satan's offer of power is that Jesus embodies the text and rejects idolatry by letting God's Word define his mission and refusing to inaugurate the kingdom of God with Satan's down payment. As Jesus refuses Satan's offer of worldly power, the Spirit empowers Jesus to withstand the same temptation to idolatry that he promises to help his followers endure (Hebrews 2:18). In his book *In the Name of Jesus*, Henri Nouwen wrote, "Power offers an easy substitute for the hard task of love. It seems easier to be God than to love God, easier to control people than to love people."[1] On the mountain when he's tempted, Jesus chooses the hard task of love and proclaims to Satan that fear will not motivate his redemptive mission. Instead, everything he does will flow from obedience to his Father, who he's anchored to in love.

These days, fear is a gateway drug to idolatry, and fear of losing political power has led Christians to bow the knee to nationalism. Fear of becoming poor in a country where poverty is criminalized has enticed people to idolize money. When fear tempts us to replace God with another savior, Jesus calls us to follow him, choose love and allow the greatest commandment (love God and love people) to inform and fuel the Great Commission (make disciples). Because fear is violently opposed to love, fear of becoming irrelevant or of "being replaced" is a myopic and weak motivation for continuing Jesus' mission of making disciples.

Fear, like what Adam and Eve experienced in the garden, can entice us to reject God's partnership with him in carrying out his will and instead choose strange partners to attain what this world calls "the good life." We see this in the Gospels when the Pharisees partner with the Herodians to kill Jesus

---

[1]Henri Nouwen, *In the Name of Jesus: Reflections on Christian Leadership* (Chestnut Ridge, NY: Crossroad, 1989), 77.

(Mark 3:6) because they feared the ramifications of Jesus upsetting the status quo that gave them power. These days, politicians stoke fear and promise Christians political power over their enemies in exchange for votes.[2] Partnering with the empire "to bring revival" is not the way of Christ because mission motivated by fear of the "other" strangles love for God and for people. Making disciples means casting out fear and teaching that the love of God reaches its goal, not as we fight culture wars against perceived enemies but as we live sacrificial lives of love for others (1 John 4:12, 18).

When tested, Jesus doesn't partner with any worldly power to establish the reign of God. Instead, Jesus relies on the power of the Holy Spirit and the Word of God to reject idolatry to carry out God's mission of redemption.

Like Jesus, we're meant to receive God's Word in faith and allow it to form our affections so that love for God and people fuels our disciple-making. Fear-based methods of making disciples are problematic because what people are saved by is what they are kept by (Galatians 3:3). If we use fear, shame, or hatred to draw people to God, discipleship means keeping them afraid, ashamed, or angry.

Jesus' disciple-making strategy introduces people to a beautiful and transformative love that forms people to love and have desires like Jesus (Psalm 37:4). Empowered by the Spirit, we help people grow in spiritual maturity as we teach them how to engage in spiritual disciplines that help them see Jesus

---

[2]Donald Trump: "I'll tell you one thing: I get elected president; we're going to be saying 'merry Christmas' again. And by the way, Christianity will have power, without having to form. Because if I'm there, you're going to have plenty of power. You don't need anybody else. You're going to have somebody representing you very, very well. Remember that." Colin Campbell, "TRUMP: If I'm President, 'Christianity Will Have Power' in the US," *Business Insider,* January 23, 2016, www .businessinsider.com/donald-trump-christianity-merry-christmas-2016-1.

and create space for the Holy Spirit to progressively align their affections and values to Jesus' own. This is the long route to sanctification, but it's worth it.

JESUS EXPOSES IDOLS

Then and now, Jesus perceived that his disciples would misinterpret his kingdom, be enticed by the twin idols of power and money, and seek to remake him as a king in their image. When Jesus told a rich young ruler, "How hard it is for the rich to enter the kingdom of God!" Jesus' disciples were astonished and asked, "Who then can be saved?" because the rich young ruler was goals (see Matthew 19:16-26). Jesus heard every whispered conversation between his disciples about who would sit at his right hand when he came into his kingdom (Mark 10:35-45). And so, Jesus constantly sought to shift the idolatrous gaze of his disciples from the religious elite who "had the most important seats in the synagogues" (Mark 12:39) toward the key demographic of his kingdom—the hungry, the stranger, the sick, the prisoner, and the naked.

For Jesus' first disciples to continue his mission, they had to see Jesus with eyes of faith—as a messianic king who was also a servant. The same is true for us. As disciples, Jesus desires that we see him rightly (as a king who uses his power to serve and love) so that we will follow him rightly (as servants of God and God's people), compelled by the love of God (John 13:14-15, 34-35). How well we understand and embody what Jesus calls the kingdom of God is a major key for making disciples of Jesus and not disciples of culture.

Back in 2017, while teaching on the Gospel of Mark during a campus ministry Bible study, I watched students experience a collective aha moment when they realized that discipleship didn't mean choosing between the teachings of Jesus and their

passion for social justice. There were anti–police brutality protests on campus every week, and one of my goals was to show
the students that following Jesus was not primarily about
avoiding hell—and to introduce them to a God who cares more
about social justice than anyone (Psalm 89:14). That night, I
noticed the students were all wearing black (not uncommon
for New Yorkers, but still). When I asked why, they told me
they were planning on leaving Bible study early to go to a
protest with an all-black dress code. I said, "Before y'all go,
let's read through Mark 11 and 12."

In the Gospel of Mark, chapters 11 and 12 describe Jesus
showing his disciples how the idols of money and power have
corrupted the Jerusalem temple. As YHWH's mouthpiece, the
prophet Jeremiah regularly rebuked Israel's leaders at the
temple gates for oppressing immigrants, the poor, orphans,
and widows (Jeremiah 7:3-11). In Mark 11, Jesus continues in
Jeremiah's prophetic tradition by condemning the temple
system and the temple priests for their complicity in ex-
ploiting the poor and the Gentile pilgrims attending the
Passover festival. I read from *The Politics of Jesus* by Obery
Hendricks to explain how, "Priests received a portion of every
Temple sacrifice and offering. . . . The priestly aristocracy of
Jesus time were made wealthy by the people's Temple dues."[3]
So Jesus purifies the temple because it's no longer a house of
prayer for all nations, it's failing to bear the fruit of justice
and righteousness, and it's being formed into a "den of
robbers" (Jeremiah 7:11) by the religious ruling class. Then
Jesus tells a parable that foreshadows the costly price he will
pay for condemning the systemic injustice at the temple

---

[3]Obery M. Hendricks, *The Politics of Jesus: Rediscovering the True Revolutionary Nature of Jesus' Teachings and How They Have Been Corrupted* (New York: Doubleday,
2006), 115-16.

(Mark 12:1-12), and finally points out a poor widow who gives her last dime to a temple system that according to Levitical law should support her, but instead is "devouring widows houses" (Mark 12:38-44).

The students told me they'd usually heard this passage taught as an exhortation for disciples to be cheerful givers like the widow, but now they saw Jesus teaching his disciples that following him means being in solidarity with and advocating for the least of these. We discussed how Jesus sees us in our (spiritual and physical) poverty, like the widow at the temple, and unites himself with us to save us and make us whole. And in the same way, we're called to follow Jesus in seeing and treating people (who lack social capital) and their "needs as holy"[4] and live in solidarity with them. As we studied Mark's Gospel, disciples were made as they realized that following Jesus didn't mean abandoning their desire to be in solidarity with and advocate for the marginalized and oppressed.

They left Bible study that night and headed to the protest. The next morning one of them texted me to say that after the protest, she joined a small group of students who formed a prayer circle on the steps by the Alma Mater sculpture. She said she felt like God used her to be an advocate for the oppressed, just like Jesus, and for the first time in her life, her faith was publicly embodied on campus.

My primary ministry context is millennial and Gen Z people of color who live in NYC. They're not necessarily tempted to use Christianity as a means of gaining political power but rather are disillusioned by Christians who, in their words, "try to force Christian values down people's throats through

---

[4]Hendricks, *The Politics of Jesus*, 123.

political legislation." And so in my discipleship class, I teach that Jesus inaugurates and populates the kingdom of God not by force but through tangible, radical love in a cultural context of colonization and oppression that is very similar to ours.

The Christians I disciple are rightly enraged at the way systemic injustice, white supremacy, homophobia, and sexism are tolerated, and in some cases celebrated, in Christian circles. In my discipleship class we discuss what it looks like to follow Jesus, considering this unfortunate truth. As a member of an oppressed people, Jesus didn't use his power to establish his kingdom through a violent overthrow of his Roman colonizers, to the chagrin of some disciples (see John 6:15). Conversely, Jesus doesn't build his kingdom by cozying up to the elite. When Jesus extends compassion to the son of a Roman soldier (Matthew 8:5-13) he doesn't ask the soldier to handle his enemies in return. When Jesus ministers to rich men like Zacchaeus or Nicodemus, he doesn't ask for a kickback or throw a press conference to signal his proximity to power. Jesus' kingdom is different.

I was introduced to the phrase "kin-dom of God" through the writings of theologian and scholar Dr. Ada Maria Isasi-Diaz, who does not use the phrase "kingdom of God" in her writing and teaching. In her book *Mujerista Theology,* Isasi-Diaz writes, "The concept of kingdom in our world today is both hierarchical and elitist—as is the word reign." Instead, she uses the term *kin-dom* to describe the "salvific act of God" that brings "salvation and liberation" through Jesus. Isasi-Diaz continues,

> The coming of the kin-dom of God has to do with a coming together of peoples, with no one being excluded and at the expense of no one. . . . The unfolding of the kin-dom of God happens when instead of working to

become part of structures of exclusion we struggle to do away with such structures.[5]

From a Christian perspective the goal of solidarity is to participate in the ongoing process of liberation through which we Christians become a significantly positive force in the unfolding of the kin-dom of God. At the center of the unfolding of the kin-dom is the salvific act of God. Salvation and liberation are interconnected. Salvation is gratuitously given by God; it flows from the very essence of God: love.[6]

Jesus didn't bring charity to (spiritually and economically) poor people that he encountered, but instead pursues solidarity with all people and in love tethers himself to humanity to rescue us from slavery to sin and grant eternal life. Jesus pours out his Spirit to empower us to follow him by living in solidarity with the poor and oppressed, as children of God who hunger for more kingdom siblings. I've got to be honest, when I first heard the term *kin-dom* I was like, "She's doing a lot," but the more I thought about it, *kin-dom* is a more accurate way to describe the organic, familial community of the redeemed than the word *kingdom*, which has so much historically awful baggage.

Author and historian Dr. Diana Butler Bass writes about how the story many Christians tell themselves about Jesus' kingship leads to lovelessness and idolatry. She says, "Christians haven't done too well with kingship—not in history and not now. We've far too often desired our own Jesus-Caesar to kick earthly kings and emperors in the teeth. We've wanted our Jesus, our version of Christ to triumph politically and

---

[5]Ada Maria Isasi-Diaz, *Mujerista Theology: A Theology for the Twenty-First Century* (Maryknoll, NY: Orbis Books), 65-66.
[6]Isasi-Diaz, *Mujerista Theology*, 88.

execute not justice but vengeance."[7] Jesus calls his new way of living a "kingdom," not so his disciples can domineer over others but to juxtapose it with the colonizing Roman Empire that his people are in subjugation to. Jesus reveals how under God's saving rule, discipleship leads to corporate liberation (John 8:36). From demon-possessed men to ceremonially unclean women, Jesus makes disciples out of people who are relegated to social isolation because Jesus' kingdom is a place where family is redefined. As Jesus heals lepers he restores them to community (Luke 5:12-14), and the discarded and rejected become children of the King. Jesus refers to his disciples not as subjects but as kin—as family (Mark 3:34-35)—and, in his humanity, Jesus is our older brother who shows us how to be the obedient children of God that God intended us to be (Hebrews 2:11, 14).

Jesus' kingdom is a place of shared resources (Matthew 10:8) because it's empowered by the love that a shared Spirit produces. The kingdom of God is good news to the outcast, a place where the brokenhearted are met with compassion and healing, and a place of freedom from idolatry and a fear-based scarcity mindset. It's a non-hierarchal community of mutuality that people can't force themselves or anyone else into (Matthew 11:12; John 3:5). And the cost of the passport to the kingdom has been purchased by Jesus, to keep Christ-followers from becoming arrogant kingdom gatekeepers.

Because inflation is the devil, I regularly find myself at a local food pantry in Brooklyn. Every week Pastor Sharmaine (who runs the pantry) works miracles with donated food. On a recent visit, I pulled up and there was a full-blown fight happening

---

[7]Diana Butler Bass, "Sunday Musings: King Jesus. Really?" The Cottage, November 20, 2022, https://dianabutlerbass.substack.com/p/sunday-musings-ea7.

between some of the pantry regulars and a group of thirty Latino men I'd never seen before at the pantry. A woman standing nearby said to me, "They skipped the line! I can't believe they're serving them before us." Pastor Sharmaine and a few volunteers separated the new group of men from the rest of us and after a semblance of order was restored, she came over to us regulars and shout-whispered, "I know y'all been waiting. But these men don't have anything! They're migrants and I'm going to serve them first. Don't worry, there's enough for everyone."

I can't speak for everyone in that line, but in that moment, my US citizenship didn't taste like privilege, because I didn't think there would be enough.

So, we waited.

Turns out Pastor Sharmaine knew something about God being a provider. About fifteen minutes later, a car drove up with sandwiches that were given out to the group of men, and us regulars got our usual bag of groceries. As I headed home with a frozen Cornish hen, a loaf of bread, and fresh vegetables spilling out of my bag, I thought about how Pastor Sharmaine combated the scarcity mindset that prevents us from living out embodied love for our neighbor.

In her essay "Solidarity: Love of Neighbor in the Twenty-First Century," Isasi-Diaz writes, "My work is not a doing for others but a being with others. My goal is not to be like the poor and oppressed, but rather to be in solidarity with them."[8] For most of my life solidarity with the poor meant giving whatever I could (money for a meal, a MetroCard swipe, the address of a local shelter) to someone less fortunate. But in New York City, where I learned from a young age to avoid the "empty" subway car, and where a homeless man was recently

---

[8]Isasi-Diaz, *Mujerista Theology*, 86.

strangled to death on the subway for the "crime" of begging for food and water,[9] I'm learning that solidarity with the poor is much more than charity, and it can't mean aligning my fortunes with the status quo. Jesus didn't simply have sympathy for poor people, Jesus became poor and was good news to the poor (2 Corinthians 8:9).

Jesus knew that advocating for the oppressed would get him killed and he did it anyway (Mark 11:17-18). I often ask myself, If baby Jesus were born in New York City, would his manger have been destroyed in a homeless encampment sweep? If solidarity with humanity cost Jesus his life, what should it cost us? Maybe it costs us comfort as we ask ourselves if we'd welcome or try to block a homeless shelter being built in our neighborhood. How can solidarity with the poor help us embody our discipleship, reflect the already-but-not-yet kingdom, and be a "we do" lesson that we can invite other disciples into? I don't have the answers, but I do know that solidarity should cost us something and that following Jesus must shape how we use our power to love. If peoples' hearts can be shaped by racist propaganda, who, what, and how we love can also be recalibrated by what James K. A. Smith calls "counter liturgies—embodied, communal practices that are loaded with the gospel."[10] This is good news for the church.

A RECONCILED KIN-DOM

We make disciples when we invite people to "taste and see" that the Lord is good at Jesus' table of abundance because the kingdom of God is like a potluck dinner party where you come

---

[9]Jaclyn Diaz, "Daniel Penny Is Charged with Second-Degree Manslaughter in the Death of Jordan Neely," NPR, May 12, 2023, www.npr.org/2023/05/12/1175776831 /daniel-penny-criminal-charges-jordan-neely-death-chokehold.

[10]James K. A. Smith, *You Are What You Love: The Spiritual Power of Habit* (Grand Rapids, MI: Brazos Press, 2016), 57-58.

empty-handed but leave with a full belly and spirit. By the power of the Holy Spirit, our churches should look increasingly like a dinner party that doesn't make sense to the watching world. I think Jesus' pièce de résistance is the multiethnic, reconciled, and reconciling community of the redeemed, and we're called to join in the growth plan by making disciples (Ephesians 2:10).

Because making disciples is a continuation of the reconciliatory mission of Christ (Colossians 1:20), a beautiful result is the deep friendships with people that I wouldn't be friends with if I weren't a Christian. I live in NYC, which is very diverse but extremely racially segregated.[11] I was recently invited by a friend to preach at a women's retreat hosted by a predominately Korean American church, and while I was talking with some women after my sermon, one of them asked me, "Do you still believe Jesus works miracles like we see in the Bible?" I told her, "The fact that I'm the keynote speaker of this retreat is a miracle!" Growing up in Brooklyn in the 1980s, I regularly saw Black people order Chinese food through bulletproof glass partitions and mock the accents of the Chinese owners of those restaurants. As an adolescent, I was regularly followed and accused of stealing by Asian owners of beauty supply stores. Art imitated life in movies like Spike Lee's *Do the Right Thing*, which illustrated how there was no love lost between Black people and Asian American immigrants in NYC in '80s and '90s.

Some forty years later, when I hang out with my Chinese American friend Ava, we still get looks from people that seem

---

[11]Danielle Cohen, "NYC School Segregation Report Card: Still Last, Action Needed Now," UCLA Civil Rights Project, www.civilrightsproject.ucla.edu/research/k-12 -education/integration-and-diversity/nyc-school-segregation-report-card-still-last -action-needed-now.

to say, "How do they know each other?" Apart from the Holy Spirit, Ava and I don't have much in common. I'm an African American woman born and raised in Brooklyn, and she's a Taiwanese woman who immigrated to California with her family as a child. We became friends while working in campus ministry together, and now I call her family. Ava and I both have children, and once day while discussing how we navigate the "oppression Olympics" that can happen between racial minorities in the United States, she said, "I recognize that your Black sons will be looked at as dangerous even though they're not, but my Asian son will always be seen as 'the other.'" I looked at her like she was crazy and said, "I'd much rather my son be seen as 'the other' than potentially be unjustly murdered because Black skin is perceived as dangerous." She said, "I guess my son's problem is a safer one to have, but it's still messed up." And then we had an awkward but dope conversation about how white supremacy pits "model minorities" against African Americans. We don't talk about racism every time we get together, but when we do, I think about how attractive the body of Christ would be to a watching world if more Christians had the "you can babysit my kids" type of friendship with all kinds of people, and if we took time to be honest about, interrogate, and repent for our biases face to face. I think it would be a healthier body, one that we wouldn't be ashamed to invite people into, and one that represents the messy but beautiful kingdom of God.

5

HOW DO WE MAKE DISCIPLES?

WE "MAKE DISCIPLES" OF JESUS in the same way that my sons (aged six and ten) "make cookies" with me. I buy the ingredients, find the mixing bowls, preheat the oven, explain the recipe, and then we work together to make something beautiful. Do I provide the context for the cookies to be made? It's my kitchen. Do my children make a mess most times? Absolutely! In the kitchen sometimes my sons deviate from my instructions, but as we work together, something delicious is made. In the same way, the sacred work of making disciples is initiated by God, empowered by the Holy Spirit, and an invitation to continue in the work of Jesus. When Jesus proclaimed, "I am the gate; whoever enters through me will be saved" (John 10:9), he announced that he was replacing the temple as the place where people would encounter God. When the early disciples continue the story of Jesus and proclaim healing (outside the temple gates) in the name of Jesus, we see the active presence of God (the Holy Spirit) at work in regular people in regular places (Acts 3:6). Empowered by the Holy Spirit, we make disciples as we introduce people to Jesus Christ, who makes God known.

THE RECIPE

Even if my kids never become world class pastry chefs, I love being with and working with them while we stir and fold and mix, no matter the mess. I could bake much more efficiently alone, but what fun would that be? If you're reading this book and are doubting your ability to make disciples, be encouraged—making disciples is a group project that Jesus happily invites us into (John 12:26). The Father is the author of salvation (Psalm 118:14; Hebrews 12:2), Jesus provides the recipe of a sacrificial life of love and obedience, and the Holy Spirit empowers us to share Jesus' recipe with others. Out of our union with Christ flows a life laid down in the service of others (enemies included). In short, we meet Jesus, and Jesus gives us new affections by his Spirit so that we desire to introduce people to Jesus and his way of living. This introduction looks like preaching the good news of the kingdom (with our life and lips) by the power of the Holy Spirit sent from God (Acts 1:8). If this makes you nervous, look at the advice Jesus gave his disciples about making disciples and sharing the good news of the gospel:

> Just say whatever is given you at the time, for it is not you speaking, but the Holy Spirit. (Mark 13:11)

> When you are brought before synagogues, rulers and authorities, do not worry about how you will defend yourselves or what you will say, for the Holy Spirit will teach you at that time what you should say. (Luke 12:12)

The same Spirit that empowered Jesus for ministry empowers us to proclaim the good news of redemption and eternal life that is offered in Jesus because the Holy Spirit is Jesus' hype man (John 15:26). The same Holy Spirit that applied the gospel to your heart will do the same for someone else.

LET'S GET PRACTICAL

There are many ways to share the good news of the gospel of Jesus Christ with people, and all of them require taking time to get to know the people we're sharing the gospel with. If I'm getting to know someone and I learn that they come from a shame-based culture where people pleasing is rewarded, I emphasize the lavish grace that Jesus offers. I tell people who tell me they hate going to church that Jesus did some of his best healing in the streets. If I'm talking with someone who struggles with bondage to an addiction, I share that I am the prisoner that Jesus came to set free (Luke 4:18). And if they let me, I talk about my addiction to drugs and how I was set free to a healthy relationship with my body through a relationship with Jesus. If I'm talking to someone who is cynical and fed up with the wicked people and systems in the world, I emphasize the power of the gospel to make all things new (2 Corinthians 5:17).

When I was in my early twenties, my friends and I used to "evangelize" wherever we were and recite a variation of the following in the NYC metro area: "The Bible teaches that everyone is born in sin and shaped in iniquity, and we all deserve hell because of our sin. That includes you. The good news is that if you accept Jesus as your personal Savior, you can be saved from eternal damnation in hell. You can do that today." Surprise, surprise . . . people didn't always receive this as good news. Once we got chased out of a Crown Fried Chicken by a group of street pharmacists who were annoyed by our "gospel presentation" in their place of business. That night I rode the subway home rejoicing that I'd been counted worthy to suffer persecution for Jesus. I promise you there was no persecution. We were enthusiastically reciting a script that we hoped would cause heart change in people we didn't know. Good news is good to us because it has direct implications for our lives that we can see. For instance, student debt cancellation is good news because most people understand how financial debt affects every aspect of life (where we live, how we raise our children, what schools we choose to attend, what careers we pursue, and so on). We understand that debt cancellation is good news because it frees us from slavery to our debt and gives us financial freedom in our decision-making.

We follow in Jesus' footsteps when we share the good news of the gospel in a way that helps people see the direct implications of that good news on their vertical relationship with God and horizontal relationships with the rest of creation. The good news of the gospel is in Jesus. God restores "every relationship that was broken by humanity's choosing its own way to peace."[1] We live in a messed-up world. The good news of the gospel isn't only that Jesus atones for our sins but also that, in Jesus, God stepped into the wilderness of this world in a physical body to fix what was broken by showing humans how to live in this broken world as obedient sons and daughters of God. Jesus was in this actual world in an actual body, loving actual people, and that same Jesus calls deeply flawed people into relationship to follow him so that he can re-create us in his image for the flourishing of the world.

In Genesis 3:9-10, the Bible says, "The LORD God called to the man 'Where are you?' He answered, 'I heard you in the garden, and I was afraid because I was naked; so I hid.'" When God asks the man, where are you? He's not asking for the human's physical location. In my sanctified imagination, I hear God asking the human, "Why aren't you with me? Why is my

---

[1]Lisa Sharon Harper, *The Very Good Gospel: How Everything Wrong Can Be Made Right* (Colorado Springs, CO: WaterBrook Press, 2016), 123.

presence a problem? You should be with me! That's why I created you." The gospel is good news because it reveals God's commitment to answer his own "Where are you?" question and in Jesus restore us back to fellowship with God. The gospel shows us that God's desire for us is greater than sin's desire for us (Genesis 4:6-7). In her book *The Very Good Gospel*, Lisa Sharon Harper writes that all of Scripture "is the story of God's work to redeem the very goodness of all creation and to restore shalom on earth—all through the power of radical love."[2]

God can meet us anywhere. I was recently at a friend's birthday party and someone engaged me in a conversation about my ministry work. People don't always like to talk about religion at parties; however, she was intrigued. As I answered her questions about work at my local church, tears welled up in her eyes. I handed her a napkin from the bar. She said, "I'm sorry, but as you've been talking about how you help people follow Jesus, it made me realize I miss God." She paused and continued, "I grew up going to church in Florida. But after Trump got elected, I couldn't stay. So, I left church. It was hard, but politics turned my church into a place that I didn't recognize. But you know what? None of those people reached out after I left. Not one. I was so angry. But I miss them." I said, "You do?" She said, "I don't miss the politics, but I miss this! I miss talking to people about Jesus. I haven't been back to church since I moved to NYC. Tonight is the first time in a long while that I realized how much I miss God." We exchanged contact information, and I said, "I'm not sure you'll ever feel comfortable going back to church. But I'm glad you experienced the love of God tonight. Just because you left church, doesn't mean that God left you

---

[2]Harper, *Very Good Gospel*, 51.

because God lives within you." We embraced and she promised to visit my church. Whether she ever visits or not, we rejoiced that night over the good news that God's grace and mercy can follow us wherever we go and that God's presence and power aren't limited to a church building or to a Sunday morning sermon.

We follow in Jesus' footsteps when we share the gospel in a way that shows people not just what they are saved from—Who cares about going to hell if life is already hell?—but illustrates to people the abundant life they are saved to (John 10:10). One of the things I noticed about my friend Ariyan during my internship in Los Angeles was that the palpable joy she had as a disciple of Christ reflected the abundant life that Jesus talked about, and it was attractive.

Our posture when sharing the gospel must reflect the shape of our salvation. In other words, our lives should embody the good news we share. If we're saved by grace, we should be generous with the grace we extend.

When people tell me, "It's hard for me to worship a God who allows so much suffering and pain," most times they've experienced something extremely painful or know someone who has experienced deep suffering. And so, before I quote Scripture and say, "Jesus is our high priest who can empathize with you in your weakness," I need to embody the good news of the gospel by empathizing with them and sharing in their suffering as Jesus would. We can always show people better than we can tell people.

A good way to equip yourself to share the gospel of Jesus Christ is to read through the New Testament Gospels and study "the recipe" of how Jesus engaged people. This helps us to filter out legalism that can burden people with behavior modification tactics instead of introducing them to the burden bearer.

Jesus addresses the personal, social, and cultural commitments of people he engages. We follow Jesus as we listen and learn what people's core concerns are so that we articulate the good news of the kingdom in a way that addresses those concerns. This might take months or years. That's okay. Our job is to love people, bear witness to the life and love of Jesus, and let the Holy Spirit do the rest.

When I worked in campus ministry, I remember talking with a student who, in her own words, "had one foot in the church and one foot out the door." She was leaning toward the door. She said the Bible wasn't relevant to her life, but as I got to know her, I learned that she was passionate about environmental science and the issue of climate change, and that those passions gave her purpose. Over time I was able to share with her how the gospel of Jesus Christ addressed her core concerns about the environment that she saw as part of her life's calling. We dug into Genesis 2:15 and saw how God's creational intent was for humanity to "protect and serve" the earth, but because of sin people exploit the land because "cash rules everything around me." So much so that creation groans as it waits to be set free from bondage to corruption (see Romans 8:18-25). We cracked open *The Very Good Gospel* and read about how Jesus fulfilled the original mandate from Genesis 2:15 and didn't use his power to exploit but "exercised dominion over creation to serve humanity."[3] And she began to see the gospel not as something irrelevant to her core concern about humanity's responsibility to care for the earth, but as something that could provide a sacred motivation for that concern. That student eventually came to faith in Christ.

---

[3]Harper, *The Very Good Gospel*, 113.

Finally, Jesus taught that love is how people discern that we're following him. Love for God and people must be the motivation behind anything we claim to do in Jesus' name (John 13:34-35). Love is what helps us to follow in Jesus' footsteps and make disciples because love is what motivated Jesus to be our salvation (John 3:16). Read the words of the apostle Paul as he describes his motivation to make disciples:

> Christ's love compels us, because we are convinced that one died for all, and therefore all died. And he died for all, that those who live should no longer live for themselves but for him who died for them and was raised again. (2 Corinthians 5:14-15)

The love of Jesus was the motivating force that fueled Paul's apostolic mission. I point this out because fear of rejection, fear of being associated with racist Christians, and fear of sounding foolish keeps Christians from sharing the gospel and making disciples. Paul writes that the love of Jesus (which changed Paul's story) is what motivates him to continue the mission of Jesus and make disciples. The same must be true for us. Love for God and people will cause you to care more about the person you share the gospel with than if you stumble over your words while testifying about the love of Jesus. Why? Because love crushes fear (1 John 4:18). Spirit-empowered faith is how we join Jesus in his mission to make disciples as we wait for Christ's return. Spirit-empowered faith expressing itself through love for others is how we enjoy the wait (Galatians 5:5-6).

THE POWER TO MAKE DISCIPLES

Our intimate and abiding relationship with Jesus is what fuels and empowers regular degular people like you and me to "make disciples." As Christ abides in us through the Holy Spirit, and his affections become ours, we are empowered to live in a way that reflects the truth, beauty, and goodness of God. This is what Jesus means when he says to his disciples, "Surely I am with you always" (Matthew 28:20). God's gospel of grace is pardon for the sinner and power for the sinner to follow in Jesus' footsteps (1 Corinthians 15:10; Romans 1:16).

Theologian Richard Bauckham calls this relationship "in-one-anotherness." Bauckham says, "As the love between the Father and Son overflows into the world, the *in-one-anotherness* of the Father and Son becomes the source of the *in-one-anotherness* of Jesus and the believer."[4] The more Jesus is at home in us, the more we are influenced by his Spirit and by his life (John 15:4-5). As Jesus' Spirit aligns our affections with his, we're beautified from the inside out, and we increasingly love who and what Jesus loves. We become like *The Picture of Dorian Gray* but in reverse. As we experience the transforming power of the Holy Spirit in our own lives, we increasingly reflect the values of the kingdom of God in our lives, and by God's grace people are attracted to that way of life. It's a holy collaboration.

SO, WHAT NOW?

Let's say you share the good news of the gospel with someone, and they say, "I want to follow Jesus. Where do I begin?" This is usually when we introduce them to our pastor or some other "professional Christian." This might be convenient, but it's a great way to get your pastor to resign or to turn to booze. Your pastor can't disciple everybody.

---

[4]Richard Bauckham, *Gospel of Glory: Major Themes in Johannine Theology* (Grand Rapids, MI: Baker Academic, 2015), 10-11, 13.

So, what do we do? We want the affections of Christ to be "formed" in people (Galatians 4:19). But how do we equip newish Christ-followers to walk in their God-given calling as building blocks of the temple of the Holy Spirit and embody the love of Jesus? How can we walk alongside people and help them grow into mature members of the body of Christ (Ephesians 4:15)? And how do we do it in a way that doesn't burn us out?

GOSPEL PARTNERSHIPS

Many Christians aren't familiar with the word *discipleship* (because it's churchy). Those who are familiar may view it is as an awkward weekly meetup where "baby Christians" have coffee with "solid Christians" who drop knowledge, listen to confessed sin, and teach doctrine. A hierarchical discipleship model can create a God complex in mentors and codependence in mentees, and quite frankly, Jesus rejected it (Matthew 20:20-28).

In Matthew 23:8-12, Jesus teaches that his disciples are classmates in the school of Jesus Christ. In other words, Jesus calls all disciples (seasoned and brand new) to learn from him as we make disciples (John 14:12). In their book *Urban Ministry*, Harvie Conn and Manuel Ortiz write about the importance of mutuality in ministry. They write, "We are in need of each other. We are to exercise our spiritual gifts out of mutual concern and submit to one another as we yield to God's lordship (Eph 5:21). In other words, Christian living and growth takes place in reciprocity, as we build relationships."[5]

The more I study the Pauline epistles, the more I see the reciprocity between the apostle Paul and the Christian communities that he disciples and teaches. For example, the love

---

[5]Harvie M. Conn and Manuel Ortiz, *Urban Ministry: The Kingdom, the City, and the People of God*, (Downers Grove, IL: InterVarsity Press, 2015), 439.

that flows from the Holy Spirit sustains Paul's relationship with the Philippian church and empowers Paul to engage in "socially distanced discipleship," lovingly encouraging them through a letter. But the ministry isn't just one way. Because of what Paul and the Philippian church share—namely, the Holy Spirit—the ministry flows in both directions. Roughly ten years after he planted the church in Philippi, Paul wrote this to them:

> I thank my God every time I remember you. In all my prayers for all of you, I always pray with joy because of your partnership in the gospel from the first day until now, being confident of this, that he who began a good work in you will carry it on to completion until the day of Christ Jesus.
>
> It is right for me to feel this way about all of you, since I have you in my heart and, whether I am in chains or defending and confirming the gospel, all of you share in God's grace with me. God can testify how I long for all of you with the affection of Christ Jesus. (Philippians 1:3-8)

In Philippians, the Greek word *koinōnia* is translated as "sharing," "partnership," "communion," and "fellowship in the gospel," and it expresses the mutuality in the relationship between Paul and the Philippian church. Paul views his relationship with that community of disciples as a "gospel partnership" (*koinōnia*) that he is grateful for, not a hierarchical construct that places him on an apostolic pedestal with the Philippians beneath him (Philippians 1:5). Their symbiotic relationship is key to the joy and sustenance of the apostle and the church (Philippians 1:4-5; 2:25), and it can also inform how we view making disciples in the local church.

Empowered by the Spirit, the Philippian church reminds Paul that he is loved. If they can help it, he will not bear his

burdens alone (Philippians 4:16). The Philippian church finan-
cially supports Paul (Philippians 4:16), and after he's put on
house arrest, they send a financial gift by way of a church
member named Epaphroditus (Philippians 2:25). Paul responds to their generosity with this epic thank-you letter,
where he reminds them that God's work of grace toward them
is not in vain, and that it will reach its goal in their lives even
during suffering. There is a healthy mutuality of care and
burden-bearing between these gospel partners, fueled by the
grace and love of Christ. Their gospel partnership is based on
what they have in common, which informs their joy and
mutual growth in Christlikeness. They share in the grace of
God (Philippians 1:7), they share Paul's troubles (Philippians
4:14), and they share in the comfort and compassion of God by
virtue of their union with Christ (Philippians 2:1-4).

Teaching through Philippians and discovering the beauty of
the reciprocal nature of this gospel partnership changed how
I viewed discipleship ministry. For many years, the only model
I knew for mentoring was a hierarchical one, where all the
teaching, exhortation, and encouragement was expected to
flow in one direction, from mentor to mentee. This was
harmful in practice because it made me feel like I couldn't
share my doubts, weariness, and fears with someone I was
discipling. I worried that if they saw me struggle they would
assume, "Yolanda is a leader and if she's struggling in her faith,
then what hope is there for me?" How prideful of me!

When we only pour out in ministry, without being poured
into, we say "I don't need you" to our brothers and sisters
(1 Corinthians 12:21) and rob ourselves of a vital means of
God's grace. God freely and lavishly pours out his Spirit on the
body of Christ so we can use our spiritual gifts to serve and
build up the body of Christ. Many times at the end of a

conversation, I'll ask a mentee to pray for me because I need it but also because it creates a context for them to imitate Jesus, grow in spiritual maturity, and embody the gospel as they "bear my burdens" in prayer.

In the same way, Paul acknowledges his weakness to the Philippian church and invites them to share in his suffering and to pray for him (Philippians 1:19). Paul is honest with the Philippians about his emotional state and anxiety (Philippians 2:28). When he writes, "I know that through your prayers and God's provision of the Spirit of Jesus Christ what has happened to me will turn out for my deliverance. . . . I eagerly expect and hope that . . . I will have sufficient courage so that Christ will be exalted in my body, whether by life or by death," there's a blend of vulnerability and confidence in the Holy Spirit and in their prayers on his behalf. Paul doesn't minimize his suffering to protect the Philippians but allows them to bear his burdens as the Spirit empowers them. Like Paul, we need to view discipleship relationships as holy collaborations that sustain us and enliven our faith even as we mentor people who are newer to following Jesus than we are.

Ironically, Paul's gospel partnership creates an opportunity for the Philippians to embody kingdom values and follow Jesus' teaching to care for the "least of these" as they send Paul aid while he's on house arrest (see Matthew 25:34-36, 45). Like Jesus, the Philippian church and Epaphroditus are "good news to the poor" as they care for Paul! After ten years of ministry, Paul is the recipient of the fruit of the gospel growth of the Philippian church and is sustained by that fruit.

The Philippians are not codependent and, despite his apostolic pedigree, Paul has no weird God complex (Philippians 3:3-8) because Paul knows that God—and not him—is working in the Philippians to fulfill his good purpose

(Philippians 2:13). Paul knows that God—not him—will supply their needs according to the riches of his glory (Philippians 4:19). What a relief to know that God is ultimately in control of the sanctification and the gospel growth of the people we mentor. The Holy Spirit empowers our ability to embody Jesus' virtues and make disciples. Remembering this should humble us and keep our mentoring relationships from becoming codependent and hierarchical.

As the people I mentor experience me teaching them how to study and apply God's Word, they usually seek to imitate what they see me do. This is tricky because the goal is for us to help people we're discipling grow as they follow Jesus, not us. If you're a good mentor, and a little bit charismatic, people will try to put you on a pedestal. Remind them that you're not goals—Jesus is. Remind them that the Holy Spirit, who lives in you, lives within them too. People are grateful to have someone to help them interpret the Word and to provide spiritual guidance, and that's not a problem. It is a problem when we're tempted to forget that, unlike the world we live in, there's no hierarchy in the kingdom of God—we're all priests.

6
SERVANTS, ANSWER THE CALL

OVER THE PAST TWENTY YEARS I've worked both formally and informally in ministry, and as an extrovert's extrovert, I love getting to know people. One type of person I often come across is what I would call "busy but bored" Christians. They serve in local church ministries but feel like their Christian walk is ashy and dry. They reminisce about how exciting discipleship felt when they first met Jesus and wish they could go back in time. This is the group I seek out and equip to make disciples. I've been in this group. To my fellow group members, this chapter is for you.

After graduating from college, I returned to Brooklyn and eventually joined a weeknight discipleship class that my pastor, the Rev. Alvin Bernstine, taught at my home church. My new job required me to work on Sundays, and I was grateful to have a place to grow in spiritual maturity despite missing Sunday service. I'd recently committed to reading the Bible straight through (from Genesis to Revelation) for the first time and had just quit smoking weed for the third time. Once the discipleship class ended, I was no longer working weekends. Rev. Bernstine found out and asked me to pray about volunteering with the youth ministry and teaching the high school Sunday school class at church. To say I was shook is an understatement. I felt like a preschool Christian, but I said yes.

When I began teaching the class, I loved figuring out ways to make the Bible come alive for these teens every Sunday morning. But after a few groggy (possibly hung-over) Sunday mornings, I realized my Saturday night routine had to switch from late nights at the club with friends to creating Bible study lessons that would engage the teens and demystify churchy concepts. As I got to know them, I learned that many of them were wrestling with hard relationships with parents, siblings, and friends. One Saturday night I decided to use the lyrics to Eminem's "Cleaning Out My Closet" to lead a discussion on Christ's command to love our enemies and what that meant for difficult relationships. They loved it.

I recall sitting around a table in a small room above the sanctuary, marveling at their thoughtful conversations at 9:30 on Sunday mornings and seeing their eyes light up with the joy that came with understanding Jesus' words for themselves. Serving them ignited a passion in me for teaching the Scriptures that I previously hadn't known existed, and it taught me so much about what it meant to be a leader. Being a leader meant sacrifice. Choosing to spend my Saturday nights praying for wisdom and creating relatable lessons instead of going out clubbing was more about being a good steward of my time than about not drinking. Over time my motivation to serve them began to shift from teaching so that God would be pleased with me to teaching to introduce them to my friend Jesus so they could experience his love for themselves.

Many times, my Gen-X pop culture references went over their heads, and sometimes they called me corny, but what mattered was that they looked for me to show up every Sunday morning, and I did. I learned to be a much better listener than talker. I learned to take the Scriptures seriously but not take myself so seriously. Discipling them didn't mean I was certain about everything concerning God and God's Word. How could I be? The Bible calls us to "correctly handle the word of truth" (2 Timothy 2:15) but if we're honest, it's impossible to believe in the God of the Bible and not be comfortable with mystery.

Back then, I thought spiritual maturity meant being always "prepared to give an answer to everyone who asks you to give the reason for the hope that you have" (1 Peter 3:15), but as I was seeking to "make disciples" of those teens, I was forced to admit that I didn't have all of the answers as to why a sovereign God would allow them to endure deep suffering in their adolescence. I couldn't answer all their questions and that messed with me. I wanted them to share my hope. I wanted to prove to them that God was worth following and that there was a biblical response to all their questions, but one morning when one of them asked me why God would allow her parents to get divorced, I said, "I don't know," and we prayed together.

Being a leader meant humbly depending on God to help me teach what I was still trying to figure out myself: Suffering and the sovereignty of God. How to balance humility and ambition. How to be a Christian and not be a jerk. I was studying the book of Romans at the time and having a context to be the "hands and feet" of Jesus every Sunday morning made the concept of being Christ's body real—to me and to the teens. We know Jesus more intimately as we embody his commands in real life situations. I'm grateful to Rev. Bernstine for giving me an opportunity to live out my faith and to depend on God to help me do what I couldn't in my own strength.

Teaching that class allowed me to share the cruciform recipe of Jesus' life that people shared with me in my childhood. Discipleship wasn't a word I heard a lot growing up. But I do remember faithful Christians like Naomi Pinkney, Roy Bratton, Josephine Harris, Carolyn Littlejohn, Minister Carol Burris-Clarke, Rev. Carl Darrisaw, Albert Hall, Mary K. Williams, Linda Collier, and Willie Watson teaching me and scores of other children about Jesus every Sunday in the wood-paneled fellowship hall of Mt. Lebanon Baptist Church. No blogs, no podcasts, no think pieces. They just showed up. They were faithful. When they sewed our costumes for Sunday school plays, made chicken box lunches for us to eat on youth retreat bus rides, or used their personal vacation time shares as the youth retreat location space, they embodied the generosity of Jesus and fulfilled his Great Commission. They served us as if they were serving God himself—and in a way, they were.

We were teenagers, but Rev. Darrisaw, who was our youth pastor, conducted "we do" discipleship lessons every month when he took us to visit the elderly "sick and shut in" members. He'd share a thought from Sunday's sermon, we'd take Communion together, and then sing a hymn to those grateful octogenarians. Even at that young age, there was something about following Christ with all our senses that was transformational. We were being discipled whether we knew it or not. Those men and women weren't perfect by any means—I once saw a Sunday school teacher cuss someone out over whose cake got put out first on the after-church dessert table—but they were faithful servants of Christ and us. Years later, as I poured into those teens the love that had been poured into me, we grew up into Christ together. I think that's what Jesus meant when he taught that disciples are different-sized branches attached to the same vine, growing together and occasionally bearing fruit.

PEER DISCIPLESHIP

As our church grew, Rev. Bernstine started multiple women's Bible studies and divided us up by age. The older women were the Sarahs, the middle-aged women were the Marthas, and the young adult women were placed in the "Rahab Group Bible Study." I know, I know. At first I was offended. Like, "Wasn't Rahab a prostitute? What is he trying to say?" But after a few weeks of attending, I started to refer to it as the "Rehab" Bible study because that's kind of what it was for me. We were mostly in our twenties, and I was excited to have a place to bring my whole self. I had so many questions about how to follow Jesus in my everyday life, how to give myself grace as I grew spiritually, and how to treat men as "brothers in Christ," and not just a means to a good time.

That Bible study provided a safe space where we could share our hopes, fears, addictions, and anxieties without fear of judgment. It felt so safe. I'd worn out my VHS copy of *No More Sheets*, and it was great to have other women to process together what it meant to be a twenty-something Christian in NYC. My good friend Ava always says that in life we balance being known and being safe. The safer you are, the less known you are, and vice versa. Back then, being myself in Christian spaces didn't always feel safe, but on Thursday nights on Bainbridge Street I was able to feel safe and be known. We read through a book called *Lord, I Want to Be Whole*, by Stormie Omartian, together, and every week a woman named Valerie would lead a discussion on one of the chapters. Valerie was intentional about the group being a place of safety and embrace. She made it clear that what we discussed in the group stayed in the group and in doing so created a space where we could "spiritually undress" and talk about the good, the bad, and the ugly . . . with no judgment. Before Valerie, I'd never seen a church leader be so transparent about their own sin and struggles. Every week as Valerie shared her life and wisdom with us, she set me free to be real about my struggles, doubts, and spiritual confusion, because in the past, I thought being publicly transparent about my spiritual doubt and sin struggles would disqualify me as a church leader.

At the end of every study, we'd close out in prayer. My God, those prayers. I grew up "saying my prayers" at night and before meals, but holding hands with those women, crying out to God for ourselves, the world, and each other, I felt like we were talking to God for real. There's a passage in Acts chapter four about a corporate prayer meeting feeling like an earthquake, and maybe Luke was being hyperbolic, but that's what our prayers felt like to me too. I felt known, challenged, and deeply loved, all at the same time. I was able to be vulnerable, be present, and struggle with other women who became like sisters to me.

A few weeks after the Bible study began, I ran into my friend Lisa inside the Broadway Junction train station in Brooklyn. We both grew up in the same church, but I hadn't seen her in years. I was like, "Yooo what's going on? Let me tell you about this Bible study!" We chatted for a bit, and I invited her to come.

A few weeks later, Lisa showed up. After we opened in prayer, Valerie asked her to share whatever was on her heart with the group. Lisa started to talk about how unbearable and abusive her home life was, and how she was "that woman" you'd see walking down the street or on the train, just crying. She shared how every day she'd be waiting for the subway on her way to work and would think to herself, *Now is the time. No one will miss you, Lisa. . . . You can just jump.*

We listened. Uninhibited, tears flowed down Lisa's cheeks. Lisa said, "I came to church the other Sunday with my mom . . . half drunk . . . I saw y'all singing praise and worship . . . y'all

looked so happy . . . and then, lo and behold, I saw Yolanda at
Broadway Junction. And so, I'm here." Valerie walked over to
Lisa, placed her hands on her shoulders, said, "Let's pray," and
began to thank and praise Jesus that Lisa came to be with us.

Lisa kept coming and it didn't take long before we became
good friends. We also became friends with Laurel and Tiffany,
two other women from the group. After work we'd meet up,
hog the big table at Bread Stuy, and spend hours talking about
God, politics, life, tryna be celibate, relationships, work, and
our dreams. It was such a relief to have people to be honest
with about my struggles with addiction. Countless conversations over lunch specials from Joya in Laurel's apartment. So
much prayer.

Years later in seminary, I learned that what I was experiencing was the church as a "charismatic, living organism, a
community of the Holy Spirit."[1] The Bible study wasn't only a
context for me to grow in my faith, but also a place for me to
experience other women telling me the truth about Jesus with
their lives.

It was family.

It was the kin-dom.

Recently, I was chilling with Lisa and Laurel. While our
children played together nearby, we reminisced about how
that Bible study community formed us some twenty years ago.
Lisa said,

> I love y'all so much. Y'all don't even know. That Rahab
> Bible study saved my life. There was so much spiritual
> warfare and abuse at home, and I had to learn how to live.
> That first night, even after I told y'all that I was suicidal,

---

[1]Howard A. Snyder, *The Community of the King* (Downers Grove, IL: InterVarsity
Press, 2004), 76.

Valerie was like, "I think you should talk to Laurel because I think her roommate moved out." I'm seeing Laurel, but I see a White girl. So, I wasn't sure. And then I talked to her, and Laurel was, "Sure dude! Sure man!" And it was life for me from that moment. All of my suicidal ideation went away. If it wasn't for me bumping into you at that train station . . . if it wasn't for that time period . . . I wouldn't be here. I found love . . . the way God made us . . . the village that we became. I'm so grateful.

The phrase "do life together" is overused in Christian circles, but that bad boy was real. I wrote earlier about how segregated NYC is, and to see a White woman (Laurel) invite a Black woman (Lisa) that she barely knew into her one-bedroom Brooklyn apartment, during peak Brooklyn gentrification years, was like seeing Jesus himself. Tiffany had moved to Brooklyn to become a star of stage and screen, and whether she was booked and busy or spritzing perfume in the cosmetics aisle at Macy's, we regularly got up to wrestle in the Word together, pray, and just hang out. We were all so different, but we shared the same Spirit, and we grew together, being built up in love as we nudged each other toward Jesus. We were a miracle.

Now, at that point in my life, I must admit, I was *that* Christian friend: Giving out gospel tracts on the subway on my way to work. Tossing my secular music into the trash and telling you about it. Posting very long Scripture passages on Myspace. If you talked to me for more than three minutes, I was hitting you with my unsolicited testimony and inviting you to some church function, whether you wanted to come or not. Shout out to my friends who tolerated my annoying "certainty about all things" discipleship stage. But by God's grace, that day in the train station Lisa saw in me a bit of what I saw in Ariyan when I was in college. At the time, I surely didn't see myself as someone to be looked up to spiritually, but you never know who is watching your life and is waiting for you to reach out. Don't be afraid.

The peer discipleship we experienced in that women's Bible study was a major key to us growing in spiritual maturity. Every week we helped each other "get dressed" with the virtues of Jesus, and we sang salvation songs to each other. We interpreted Scripture in community, and what I received in that community was poured out to the teens I'd begun to disciple and teach. We experienced the diversity, mutuality, and interdependence inside what the apostle Paul calls the body of Christ: "God has placed the parts in the body, every one of them, just as he wanted them to be. If they were all one part, where would the body be? As it is, there are many parts, but one body" (1 Corinthians 12:18-20).

As a disciple of Christ, it's vital to have safe people that you can be honest and vulnerable with. When I think about this, I'm reminded that Judas was only truly known by Satan and Jesus. No other disciples really knew Judas. Maybe if he'd been vulnerable and opened up to someone about his stealing habit, they would have gone after him when he went off to betray Jesus. Ironically, Jesus models this vulnerability when he invites the disciples to pray with him in the Garden of Gethsemane—because he was struggling. We can't be truly loved and encouraged in a way that brings about spiritual growth by people who don't know us.

Pastors spend lots of time learning the latest evangelism strategies to engage their communities with the gospel, but a healthy community of people, united in cruciform love, that newcomers can enter into and be embraced is a truly beautiful witness of the kingdom of God.

Herman Bavinck wrote, "As the church does not exist apart from Christ, so Christ does not exist without the church."[2] We make disciples by introducing people to Jesus. As people are embraced by Jesus' body, they start asking questions about the head of the body. Without the church, Jesus is a disembodied head, and without Jesus, the church has no power. Because Christ is the head of the church, like a vine is the source of a branch (John 15:5), our union with Christ gives expression to Christ's work in the world, even as he's seated at the right hand of the Father. When I saw Lisa in that train station, I don't think what she needed was to meet up with me for coffee so I could teach her what I knew about Jesus. I wasn't enough. She needed connection to a Spirit-filled community where she could bring her whole self and experience the truth about Jesus with more than one person. Years ago, my dad taught me how to garden, and one of the things he showed me was how corn and beans and squash are "companion plants" that help each other grow as they are planted around each other. Similar to Jesus' gardening metaphor in John 15:5, we're all companion plants, rooted together in the same soil, who help each other grow in spiritual maturity as we're connected to the same source of life.

One-on-one discipleship is great, but it can be too intense for people who have been traumatized by Christians. Group discipleship is easier for people to ease into and takes away the pressure of feeling like they must say something to fill the silence. Also, group discipleship allows for a diversity of cultural

---

[2]Herman Bavinck, *Reformed Dogmatics*, vol. 3, *Sin and Salvation in Christ*, ed. John Bolt and trans. John Vriend (Grand Rapids, MI: Baker Academic, 2006), 473-75.

perspectives, and for each person's spiritual gifts to operate so that no one cultural way is presented as the only way to follow Jesus. In *The Community of the King*, theologian Howard Synder says that spiritual maturity "produces diversity, and diversity brings more growth. That's the secret of the Church, the gift-bearing body."[3] In a diverse city like NYC, the diversity of spiritual gifts in the body is a vital part of a church's ability to the contextualize the proclamation of the good news for all kinds of people. In a brilliant exegesis of 1 Peter 4:10-11, Snyder explains how God's gracious gift of salvation is made visible to the world as it flows through the diverse people who make up local churches: "The pure light of God's 'manifold grace' [*charis*] . . . is then refracted as it shines through the church, as light through a prism, producing the varied, multicolored *charismata* or gifts of the Spirit."[4]

As God's grace interacts with various people and produces various giftings, the witness of the body of Christ shines beautifully. In the Rahab Group Bible Study, Lisa was the recipient of teaching gifts, hospitality gifts, administration gifts, prophetic gifts, and evangelism gifts. This is one reason why we shouldn't envy someone else's gift. Your gift of creating a detailed spreadsheet, or event planning, or being a great listener, or running a meeting, or being a great hugger is just as necessary to the flourishing of body of Christ as someone's more public gift of preaching.

In the discipleship class that I currently teach, I use a drawing (that I originally made for my ten-year-old son) to explain how the Holy Spirit works when we pray. It's a simple drawing that features a ball of squiggly lines labeled *pneuma* to represent the

---

[3]Snyder, *The Community of the King*, 147.
[4]Snyder, *The Community of the King*, 77.

Holy Spirit, a stick figure to represent us, and a cloud with a crown to represent God the Father (Romans 8:26-28). It looks like a five-year-old could have drawn it, but I have high self-esteem and it works, so I use it. Unprompted, an artistic member of our church in my discipleship class took it upon himself to upgrade my sketch and send me a copy of his version for use in future classes. I was filled with gratitude and moved to tears because I realized that his willingness to use his gift was going to complement my gift and ultimately help people grow in their prayer life. This is 1 Peter 4:10 at work. This is what I mean when I say that making disciples is a group project that requires the mutually dependent body of Christ to work together to grow.

Small group discipleship in the context of the local church is an amazing way to see the diversity of people's spiritual gifts working to beautify God's creation from the inside out. God doesn't give spiritual gifts out according to gender, social standing, ethnicity, or family pedigree. We're called to steward our gifts to serve God and his people and to be good managers of what God has entrusted to us. Spiritual gifts are not gender specific (1 Corinthians 12:1-11), and they're formed and best used in community (Romans 12:4-8). It's God's grace working within believers through the Holy Spirit that equips us to be effective servants, stewards, and shepherds in the church and ministers of reconciliation in the world (Ephesians 3:7).

Throughout Scripture, we see the triune God work together to restore what sin has marred. God the Father decrees the mission, God the Son fulfills the mission, and God the Spirit regenerates people to continue the mission of restoration. Gospel-centered communities can form and restore us or de-form and imprison us. The Rahab Group Bible Study gave me the freedom to be honest about my broken relationship with myself, so that I could experience healing and invite someone else into healing. Communities can give people permission to be honest with themselves, with God, and with others, or they can shame people into churchy prisons that masquerade as small groups. By God's grace, every community of Jesus' disciples is called to be a microcosm of the cosmic reconciliation that the triune God brings. What can we learn about making disciples from the way the triune God works? How we define the church reveals how we define its Creator. Howard Snyder writes that the church should be "a community, a koinonia that is a kind of trinitarian echo."[5] We reflect the interdependence of the Trinity as we work together to make disciples and call people to be reconciled to God and to creation. The basis for the Christian unity, which provides the context for healthy discipleship, is the triune God (Ephesians 4:4-6). This diverse unity is evangelistic and attractive and is how God's "manifold" wisdom is made known to a watching world (Ephesians 3:6, 10). The body of Christ should develop an "'ecclesiology of perichoresis' in which there is no permanent structure of subordination but overlapping patterns of relationships, so that the same person will be sometimes 'subordinate' and sometimes 'superordinate' according to the gift and graces being exercised."[6] Practically, I'd imagine this would look like sometimes the elders teach and sometime the elders are taught by lay leaders. Where the person who welcomes visitors feels empowered to pray for and over a deacon, where the person who teaches in the church nursery feels empowered to speak a word of prophecy at the prayer meeting or on Sunday morning, where, because we all share the same Spirit, our gifts flow freely for the building up of Christ's body.

---

[5]Snyder, *The Community of the King*, 57.
[6]Colin E. Gunton, *The Promise of Trinitarian Theology*, 2nd ed. (Edinburgh: T&T Clark, 1997), 80.

7

DISCIPLESHIP OR MENTORING?

IN HER GROUNDBREAKING book *Mentor for Life*, Natasha Sistrunk Robinson interchangeably uses the words *discipleship* and *mentoring*. Robinson writes, "Mentoring helps us to build trustworthy relationships as we partner with God through the transformational work of the Holy Spirit to change hearts and minds."[1] Using a more familiar word like *mentoring* can be helpful when introducing people who aren't so "churchy" to the concept of discipleship. Professionally speaking, mentoring usually looks like someone with a high level of expertise advising or training a less tenured person for the purpose of professional advancement. The goal of mentoring is that as a mentee works alongside me and observes me working, they learn how to work like me, and hopefully surpass me professionally.

Jesus teaches that his relationship with the Father must be the blueprint for his disciples' relationship with the Holy Spirit. In John 14:9–15:8, Jesus basically tells his disciples, "I work, teach, and speak in such a way that if people see me, they've

---

[1]Natasha Sistrunk Robinson, *Mentor for Life: Finding Purpose Through Intentional Discipleship* (Grand Rapids, MI: Zondervan, 2016), 46.

seen the Father because the Father lives in me and works through me. In the same way, your witness will flow from the Holy Spirit who my Father will send. The Holy Spirit will live and work in you so that when people see you bear fruit, they'll be seeing the divine life working through you" (my paraphrase). Here's how this principle worked itself out in my life.

MICROPHONE CHECK 1, 2, 1, 2

A few years after I rededicated my life to Christ in college, I discovered Christian hip-hop. A friend asked me to produce a video about an outdoor Christian hip-hop outreach concert that a pastor friend of hers was organizing in the Queens-bridge housing projects in NYC. I agreed because my friend asked me to, but my expectations were low because the idea of Christian rap sounded incredibly corny to me. And in Queensbridge? Queensbridge is the largest housing project in North America, and all I knew about that neighborhood was what I heard on Mobb Deep songs. The only outdoor Christian concerts I saw as a child were Hezekiah Walker and Love Fellowship Crusade Choir, but I guarantee you nobody in those audiences was rocking camouflage hoodies, baggy jeans, and Timberlands like they were that day in Queensbridge. I arrived at the concert, and I couldn't believe my eyes.

The Christian rap artists rhymed about the love of God in a way that was so accessible, and they were in their early twenties like me! While editing the video footage later that week, I was struck by how one of the groups at the concert, Corey Red and Precise, bragged in their rhymes about the attributes of God and not money, expensive clothing, or jewelry. But I was mostly shocked that it wasn't corny. I finished editing the concert video and kind of forgot about it, but word spread in the Christian hip-hop online community about my video, and within weeks Christian rappers and producers were inviting me to make videos of their live shows for promotional use on their Myspace pages (I'm that old).

Because God has a sense of humor, I found myself at Christian rap shows just about every weekend being discipled by a style of music that belonged to me. God is so resourceful. A few months later I caught a ride with my friend Geoff to a Christian hip-hop concert in West Philly. At the time, Geoff and I worked together at a news network, and as a budding journalist he was interested in the "story" of this underground gospel rap subgenre (as he called it). So he gave me a ride to Philly and offered to help me capture concert footage and record interviews with some of the artists. This Philly concert was different from the one in Queensbridge. First of all, everyone wasn't Black. I'd never been in a multiethnic Christian space before. And as I watched Latino, Black, White, and Korean volunteers from the host church fry and hand out hundreds of whiting sandwiches to the concertgoers in Clark Park, I saw a vision of the kingdom of God.

The simple beauty of meeting the needs of a community with free fish sandwiches and sharing the gospel of Jesus Christ over DJ Premier and J Dilla instrumentals was something I'd never seen before—in the church or in hip-hop culture. The church that organized the concert was using the recipe of Jesus' cruciform life to share the good news of the gospel. It's been said that pastors should smell like sheep. Pastor Aaron Campbell smelled like sheep and fish grease. As I waited in the sandwich line watching him place glistening pieces of whiting in between slices of bread, I listened to a skinny White guy on stage rap about something called irresistible grace over Hi-Tek's "Respiration" beat, and I wondered what alternate universe I was in. A new vision of what it meant to follow Jesus was being formed in me. When I asked Pastor Aaron about the vision behind the outreach concert, he told me that his church (Antioch Christian Fellowship) was meeting people in West Philly "where they were" and contextualizing the good news of the gospel of Jesus Christ in the familiar language of hip-hop music.

That day, I listened to songs with titles like "Saved by Grace" and "Sanctification" and was introduced to Reformed theology not by reading John Calvin but through rap music. Geoff left, but I stayed in Philly all evening. Around midnight on the last Greyhound bus back to NYC, I watched the outreach concert footage I'd captured on my little camcorder and wept in the darkness. I felt like I found my tribe. Everything changed. God used this medium that I loved (hip-hop) to spark an almost insatiable hunger in me to read and study the Bible. At another concert, I befriended a Christian rap DJ named Cassandra, who invited me to a Bible study that Pastor Aaron was teaching at his house. I developed an intimate relationship with the Chinatown bus and found myself in Philly every month to go to these concerts, attend Bible study, and buy as much Christian rap as I could. I'd pore over song lyrics in the CD liner notes with my Bible in hand because there were Scripture references in parentheses for each bar of each song!

DISCIPLED INTO CULTURE

What I didn't know was that a lot of the Christian hip-hop I liked was heavily influenced by White evangelical culture—and so I became heavily influenced by White evangelical culture. And, unfortunately for everyone who knew me, I became insufferable. I read all the books. I went to all the apologetics conferences to learn how to defend Jesus from the heretics. I read all the homeschooling blogs. I denounced topical preaching and feminism. I eventually left the Rahab Bible study and my Black Baptist church in exchange for more "solid" teaching. I even "kissed dating goodbye."

I made friends with people I met at those apologetics conferences and started visiting their churches. I'll never forget the first time someone told me at church over coffee, "I didn't know you could be a Christian and a Democrat." I recall attending a prayer meeting at a friend's church where women weren't allowed to publicly pray over the group and being told that the presence of drums in church worship were a "worldly distraction." I was told that I should be discipled by older women to grow in "biblical womanhood" based on the Pauline epistle to Titus. Encouraging young people to seek out mature mentorship is good counsel, but I sadly ended up being discipled into middle-class, White domesticity.

I was being made a disciple of culture, and when you're discipled into culture and not Christ, culture is exalted, not Christ. I remember feeling the dissonance of being taught by Christians that public schools were evil and were used to indoctrinate children, even though I knew public schools had been just fine for White Christians prior to *Brown v. Board of Education*. I was told that working outside of the home was unbiblical, even though it was illegal for Black women in my great-grandmother's generation to be "stay-at-home moms."[2] My ancestors have more in common with Hagar than with Sarah.

FORMATION IN COMMUNITY

During this time, I couldn't get enough of studying the Bible and reading books on spiritual growth. I'd be on the C train

[2]*The Greenville Daily News*, "Negro Women Put to Work," Greenville, South Carolina, October 2, 1918, www.newspapers.com/clip/38314573/negro-women-to-be-put -to-work.

headed to work reading my Bible. Then when I got to work, I was "sneak reading" A. W. Tozer books at my desk. Friends began asking me if I'd ever thought about going to seminary. Over time, Pastor Aaron became a mentor, and one afternoon after Bible study, I asked him what he thought about going to seminary, cuz I'd heard it could kill your spiritual zeal. He told me to pray for discernment, look for affordable programs, and, if I found one, to give it a try. In 2007, by God's grace I was accepted into a master's degree program that was co-located between an evangelical seminary in Pennsylvania and City Seminary of New York (CSNY) in Harlem. For the next three years, I took summer intensives in Pennsylvania and classes at CSNY on nights and weekends. CSNY gave much needed balance to my annoying "I have no questions" hyper-Calvinistic biblical worldview. After work I'd catch the A train to 125th Street, grab a Popeyes shrimp box, and study alongside Presbyterian, Pentecostal, evangelical, Baptist, nondenominational, and messianic Jewish men and women. We were Jamaican, Korean, Taiwanese, Fujianese, Indonesian, African American, and Dominican. Dr. Mark Gornik, Dr. Maria Liu Wong, and Dr. Janice McLean-Farrell stretched our Christian imaginations as we read Ugandan theologians such as Emmanuel Katongole, as well as Herman Bavinck and John Goldingay.

We read and discussed Mayan Aztec theologian Dalila Nayap-Pot's essays comparing the Old Testament Moabite Ruth to the indigenous women of Central America who, like Ruth, also had to exercise "cultural and spiritual creativity" in a patriarchal society. For the first time, I began to dream about how that Old Testament narrative could speak a word of hope to immigrants in my city, who like Ruth are trying to survive and trust God in a foreign land as an "other"—as opposed to using the book of Ruth as a primer for single women on how to "find your Boaz."

NYC was our missiology classroom. We spent time in housing projects on the Lower East Side asking Jewish, Chinese, and Puerto Rican residents, "Where is God working?," and over time my discipleship worldview evolved. I began to think about what it would mean to apply Jeremiah 29:7 to my everyday life and "seek the peace of the city," following in Jesus' footsteps as an agent of shalom. Every month we engaged in a spiritual formation practice called "pray and break bread.NYC" (PBB.NYC). A neighborhood native would teach us about the history and needs of a community and share what God was doing in that community to help inform our prayers. Then we would walk and pray, pausing as the Spirit led us. Finally, we would converge on a local mom-and-pop restaurant to "buy out the bar" in Jesus' name as a love offering to that community. We weren't in the community to hand out tracts or to "take it back for Jesus." We were there to learn how God was working in that context (to exegete the community), humbly offer up our prayers, and then be good news to that community with a tangible blessing. Everyone can't go to seminary, but taking discipleship outside of your church building and learning about the felt needs of your neighbors to seek the peace of your neighbors and neighborhoods in a nonpaternalistic way is a good spiritual formation practice.

I remember my classmate Peter led a PBB.NYC in Chinatown. Peter was a local pastor and, as we stood in Columbus Park, he explained what life was like for first-generation Chinese American teens in his youth ministry who juggled being kids, doing their parents' taxes, and translating prescriptions and bills. He showed us million-dollar condos being constructed between sagging tenement buildings and talked about how gentrification was pushing working-class families out. He told us about undocumented men who struggled with depression and alcoholism and who worked fourteen-hour days for little pay and how that affected their families.

We walked the blocks, praying in front of schools, churches, fruit stands, and basketball courts. We read Jonah, discussed his contempt for the city of Nineveh, interrogated our own anti-urban biases, and asked ourselves how we could mirror God's concern for the city in our neighborhoods. If continuing the mission of Jesus started with the assumption that God was already working in my city, then discipleship meant finding out where Jesus was already working and then joining in that work. I wasn't being discipled into a particular culture; I was being taught to embody and apply the good news of the gospel within my cultural context.

Two years into seminary, I was working the night shift as an assistant editor on a reality show, and my daily joy was volunteering at an afterschool program for teenage girls called "Sister to Sister" at a local YMCA. All the girls were first-generation Caribbean American, and my plan was to teach them the biblical womanhood curriculum I'd been working on at seminary. As I got to know them, I realized they had many of the same concerns as the first-generation Chinese American teenagers that my classmate Peter told us about on that Chinatown PBB.NYC. So, I ditched the biblical womanhood curriculum and instead we talked about how to follow Jesus while we tried to be a cultural bridge between Haiti, Jamaica, Trinidad, and NYC for their parents. We talked about what it meant to honor their parents in an emotionally healthy way and still cultivate their own identities in Christ. CSNY taught me that discipleship wasn't about facilitating be-havior modification or teaching people how to regurgitate culture war talking points. Discipleship had more to do with participating in what God was doing in the lives of those teens and pointing them to follow Jesus rather than discipling them into a cultural gender construct.

The "spiritual fruit" of love, joy, peace, gentleness, kindness, patience, goodness, faithfulness, and self-control (Galatians 5:22-23) isn't gender specific, and neither are spiritual gifts (1 Corinthians 12:1-11), but we sometimes disciple people as if they were. This produces a truncated view of what it means to follow Jesus. On this topic, Aimee Byrd writes, "In Scripture . . . we find that men and women are called together in the same mission: eternal communion with the triune God. Both men and women are called to pursue the same virtues as we await our ultimate blessedness, the beatific vision—to behold Christ."[3]

Obviously, anyone can be mentored on how to follow Jesus in situations that might present themselves to one gender more than another. At Sister to Sister, we talked about body image, how airbrushing with Photoshop is a lie, and how loving yourself only when boys compliment you isn't ideal. We dug in to Luke 10:27 and Jesus' command to "love your neighbor as yourself," discussing what it meant to love ourselves and agree with how God made us as Black women, so that we might rightly love our neighbor. But mostly our conversations were rooted in introducing these young women to Jesus and showing them how they were included in God's plan to re-create all things to reflect his glory in the world. I wanted them to know that unlike the boys at school, God unconditionally loved them with an everlasting love, and I tried to embody that love by showing up for them every afternoon and listening to their stories before heading to work a night shift. In the Gospels, Jesus echoes Jeremiah's prophetic call for Israel to seek the

---

[3]Aimee Byrd, *Recovering from Biblical Manhood and Womanhood: How the Church Needs to Rediscover Her Purpose* (Grand Rapids, MI: Zondervan, 2020), 109.

peace of the city by calling his followers to be blessed peace-makers (Matthew 5:9). During those afternoons in Flatbush, I tried to help those girls be at peace with themselves with their wide noses, with their kinky hair, with their dark brown skin—and to love themselves just like God does.

Since discipleship mentoring involves Christlike rhythms being "caught and taught," mentees will observe our lives and want to imitate certain patterns and spiritual giftings. But primarily we should encourage people to follow Jesus, not us or our cultural presences. If we don't do this, we can cause people to conflate our cultural preferences with discipleship. We end up doing harm in the name of Jesus.

If we deny that we have a culture, we'll end up trying to make disciples of our own cultural version of Christianity instead of disciples of Christ. We might tell people that to be a true Christ-follower they need to be a member of a certain political party or that one nation is God's favorite, even though the Scriptures teach that the restored kingdom of God doesn't have geopolitical borders (Amos 9:11-12). If we deny that we have a culture and deny our cultural bias, we'll become like the Judaizers in Acts 15:1-2, who taught that Gentiles had to become culturally Jewish through circumcision to become Christ-followers. Missiologist Andrew Walls wrote extensively about the folly of discipling people into culture. He wrote that if the first Gentile disciples of Christ had been discipled to become culturally Jewish, "they might have become very devout believers, but they would have had virtually no impact on their society."[4]

We show people the beauty and sufficiency of Jesus by living out the gospel and encouraging each one to follow Jesus without

---

[4]Andrew F. Walls, *The Cross-Cultural Process in Christian History: Studies in the Transmission and Reception of Faith* (Maryknoll, NY: Orbis Books, 2005), 68.

a cultural costume, so that they can go into their communities introducing others to Jesus while maintaining credibility in that community. The Caribbean American girls at the YMCA didn't need me to disciple them into White middle-class evangelical domesticity. They needed the gospel and permission to worship God in spirit and in truth as their whole cultural selves. The beauty of the gospel is its translatable nature as it transforms people within cultures but doesn't wipe out their own.

GET IN POSITION TO SERVE LIKE JESUS

Some of you might be questioning God's calling on your life to be a discipleship leader in your local church community. Let me encourage you: the clearer you are on the fact that God—and not humankind—calls and empowers people to sacrificially serve God and God's people, the more qualified you are to humbly serve God's people, with or without a leadership title.

When Jesus tells his followers, "[I] did not come to be served, but to serve" (Mark 10:45), he's explaining how, in the kingdom of God, serving *is* leading. Making disciples has little to do with using your gifts to gain clout or authority over people but has everything to do with giving your gifts away to serve:

> Jesus knew that the Father had put all things under his power, and that he had come from God and was returning to God; so he got up from the meal, took off his outer clothing, and wrapped a towel around his waist. After that, he poured water into a basin and began to wash his disciples' feet. (John 13:3-5; see also John 13:14-15)

Knowing that his authority came from the Father (and not the religious glitterati of Jerusalem) empowered Jesus to serve with humility. As he washed his disciples' feet, Jesus taught an interactive "we do" lesson (with water and a towel) that people should experience his disciples as his disciples experienced him, as servants. In Jewish culture, disciples were supposed to serve their rabbi, but Jesus embodied humility as he served them.

A good second step to following Jesus in servant leadership is taking time to "stay at the table" (spend time with Jesus) and allow Jesus to cleanse us, to heal us, and comfort us so that we can do that for others. We can't pour out of an empty vessel. The time I spent on Saturday nights prepping high school Sunday school lessons and processing and studying the Word in community in the Rahab Bible study created space for me to hear from God and be sustained and formed by the Word while praying for a heart to serve. That time prepared me to go to seminary and have my learning informed by outside-the-classroom ministry experience. No experience was more important; they were all part of God's plan to help me grow and to shape my heart to love like Jesus.

8

MEETING TOGETHER

AS LIFE-GIVING AS Sunday morning service is, it's not enough. The Sunday morning service in most churches is like the stoop or the porch of the household of faith. If you're on my stoop, technically you're at my house, but you're not inside. You could sit on my stoop for an hour and leave, and unless I'm looking out my window, I would never know you were there. In the same way, you can go to church, be entertained by the music, high-five your neighbor, and be discipled by a gospel message, but never truly connect with or get to know actual human beings.

Some of us are cool with this because we don't particularly like people. But many Christians don't have the gospel partnerships I've talked about because of distrust caused by real harm that Christians have done to them in the church. Now, there is a huge difference between refusing to be in relationship with abusive, toxic people (who masquerade as Christians) and missing out on "striving together as one for the faith of the gospel" (Philippians 1:27) because "it's easier to do this Christian thing by myself." It's not. We can't be disciples or make disciples of Christ apart from the interdependent, interconnected body of Christ. But being a part of the body of

Christ and being on a church membership roll are two different things. Inviting hurt people into the body of Christ means meeting people where they are and creating space for connection to a community of Christ-followers where people can heal from hurt, without being asked to do anything but receive. When I partner up newer people with discipleship leaders at my church, I tell them, "This person is safe, but they're not perfect." Paul used the Greek term *koinonia* to express the basic meaning of the Christian faith, a sharing in the life and death of Christ that radically creates a relationship between Christ and the believer and among believers with one another in a partnership or unity.[1] Making disciples during a time when many are cautiously and carefully considering returning to the faith means inviting people into community (not necessarily church) and the beautiful koinonia of the Spirit, however slowly they need to go.

Mentoring that sparks spiritual maturity in followers of Christ will likely take place on days other than Sunday, as we build deep, flesh-and-blood relationships with people. Many people sit through sermons and have tons of questions, but since most churches don't allow for mid-sermon Q and A, they leave church confused. Until we change how we do Sunday morning,[2] small group Bible studies, prayer groups, and one-on-one discipleship relationships are great contexts to shepherd and serve, and speak truth into people's lives. If you're reading this and have agreed to act as a shepherd and servant to people in your local Christian community, or you might like to one day, thank you.

---

[1]Trent C. Butler, ed., "Communion," *Holman Illustrated Bible Dictionary* (Nashville, TN: Holman Bible Publishers, 2003), 324.
[2]Check out the New Wine Collective for great ideas on how to do this: https://newwinecollective.org.

PREPARATION

Let's say someone asks you for spiritual guidance and wants to meet up regularly to talk about questions they have concerning the Bible. First of all, praise God that in the middle of a "loneliness epidemic" someone has the courage to open up to you! Here are some guidelines for how you might prepare to respond to Jesus' discipleship calling.

Set healthy expectations. One-on-one discipleship is beautiful, but so are structure and healthy expectations. Setting expectations for what discipleship or mentorship will be like prevents people's feelings from getting hurt and keeps our mentoring from toxicity and codependence. Healthy discipleship looks like setting expectations for duration and frequency of meetings, asking good questions, and listening well.

Resist the urge to create an elaborate discipleship curriculum from scratch. Share the Scriptures you have a firm grasp on and that have been helpful in your spiritual formation. Share books that have helped you to grow in love for God and others, and offer to read them with your mentee. Talk about what you know, but be a lifelong learner. If God is who God says God is, we can never plumb the depths of knowing God. Read outside of your denominational and theological camps and share those resources with your mentees as the Spirit leads you.

For many years I exclusively read theology and spiritual formation books written by White American Protestant men and, though many were helpful, I was woefully unprepared when I began ministering to college students of varying ethnicities and denominations. Over the past few years, I've expanded my library and discovered theologians and writers like Rev. Judy Fentress-Williams, Dr. James H. Cone, Aimee Byrd, Rev. Dr. Will Gafney, Dr. Carla Works, Dr. Chanequa

Walker-Barnes, Dr. Diana Butler Bass, Dr. Willie Jennings, Pastor Rich Villodas, and Dr. Clarice J. Martin. Reading broadly has stretched me theologically in a good way; it forces me to interrogate whether my theological convictions are culturally based or Bible based. Reading broadly has also helped me to study and apply the word to cultural issues that weren't relevant when I was in seminary more than thirteen years ago. Pray for discernment as you read, and if you find a good book, write down the authors who are referenced in the footnotes and then find those books. Repeat and build your library.

Preach the gospel to others and to yourself often. No matter how long we've been Christ-followers, we need to renew our faith by seeking God and preaching the gospel to ourselves every day, which will help us persevere as we follow Jesus. My awareness of my need for grace is directly related to how much grace I extend to the people I am mentoring. Years ago, I was arguing with my husband about something and my oldest son, who was six years old at the time, shouted, "Mommy, give Daddy grace!" As my husband and I busted out laughing, I realized that at some point in my son's life he'd heard me talk about grace, and I guess he was listening. That day he reminded me that the gospel doesn't just save; it sustains and nourishes us as disciples of Christ in the day to day. It's the never-ending power of God! Meditating on the gospel daily helps us to experience the mercy and grace of God every day (Lamentations 3:22-23). We never graduate past the gospel; it's how we start our journey with God and how we persevere throughout our lives, as we follow Jesus, making disciples by relying on the sustaining power of the Holy Spirit (Galatians 3:2-5).

Pray for and find a mentor. I know this isn't always easy—especially for women. Good mentors are usually extremely busy. But with God anything is possible. Also, don't limit your search based on ethnicity. In my late twenties, a thirty-something White woman from Canada was an amazing mentor and friend to me. She taught me so much about hospitality, as she opened her life to me to talk, apply God's Word to my life, pray with me, and basically love me. Years later, the tables turned, and I helped her understand what Jesus teaches about justice. As I transitioned from campus ministry to discipleship ministry in a local church, I prayed for a seasoned female mentor who has served in a pastoral role. God answered that prayer, and as she pastors and mentors me, I've also served her by preaching and teaching for her congregation. Mentorship will lead to gospel partnership. My mentors do for me what I do for others. They ask good questions and they listen, they're safe for me, and they're great encouragers. But most importantly, they keep me honest and ask me if I'm practicing what I preach. *Am I resting? Am I trying to be the Holy Spirit by myself?* Discipleship is giving and receiving. It's a holy collaboration—being discipled and discipling others.

Pray and ask God to help you find someone you can trust. Then look for someone who is trustworthy, honest, loving, and not a gossip. Character matters most. Look for someone who is a servant to others and is a safe person. Look for someone who prays for others, is a student of God's Word, and has taught others. They should have credibility. A good discipleship mentor is humble and is likely being mentored themselves. This shows that they understand we never stop learning and maturing in Christ and are teachable (1 Corinthians 12:12, 21).

INITIAL DISCIPLESHIP MEETING

Here are some tips for planning the first meeting with a mentee:

1. Set expectations for the duration and frequency of meetings so that mentees know how much time you can give them and how long this arrangement will last. I usually meet twice a month with people that I'm discipling so there's enough time between meetings for mentees to read and formulate questions for discussion, especially if we're doing a book study.

2. Ask, "Are you open to growth? If so, where do you feel you need to grow?" when setting discipleship goals. People don't need to have everything together (who does?), but disciples of Jesus should have teachable spirits. There is no need to chase down potential mentees. If people want to be discipled, they will find you and let you know.

3. Get to know a potential mentee by asking good questions. It's difficult to encourage someone in their faith if you don't know anything about them. The person you are discipling has taken the risk to be known by you. Don't take that lightly. Jesus' discipleship call assumes that Christ-followers are concerned about each other (John 13:34-35; 15:12-13). Hebrews 3:13 calls us to "exhort one another daily" to keep ourselves from lovelessness, but the best exhortation comes when you know people. Some of my worst moments in mentoring came when I met someone, made a hasty assessment of who they were, and began answering questions that they never asked. When you ask people how they're doing, listen. The Bible admonishes disciples of Christ to be "quick

to listen, slow to speak and slow to become angry" (James 1:19). As you listen, ask yourself: What are they worried, happy, sad, angry, fearful, or hopeful about? How do they describe their circle of friends? Do they have friends? How do they talk about their families? Listening to how they describe these things will help you learn what their beliefs and values are and help you to be a better friend to them. Questions help people get in touch with themselves and interrogate why and what they believe. Questions engage our imaginations and force us to wrestle, pray, consider who Jesus is, and what that means for who we are. You'll know it's a good question when they pause, and say, "No one's ever asked me that before!" Jesus asked amazing questions as he taught his disciples. Here are a few:

- What do you want? (John 1:38)
- Who do you say I am? (Matthew 16:15)
- Do you believe I am able to do this? (Matthew 9:28)
- Do you want to get well? (John 5:6)
- Why are you so afraid? (Matthew 8:26)
- Why did you doubt? (Matthew 14:31)
- Do you still not understand? (Mark 8:21)
- What is written in the law? How do you read it? (Luke 10:26)
- Do you love me? (John 21:15-17)

Asking good questions can help us better understand the people we're discipling and create teachable moments during conversations. Below are some examples:

- Who is Jesus, and what does that mean for you today?
- How do you think God feels about you?

- What's your relationship like with God's Word? How does it make you feel?
- When is the last time reading the Word of God or prayer changed your mind?
- What does money promise? What does God promise?
- What are you afraid of? How does the Word of God address that fear?
- Do you view your body as a help or hindrance to your spiritual growth?
- Can you make time and space for God to transform you? If so, how?

4. Model transparency. Don't expect people to do something that you don't feel comfortable doing. Be willing to confess your struggles and to repent of your own sin in meetings. This will help to break down emotional walls that someone may have up if they don't know you well. If someone has mustered up the courage to confess sin to you, honor their vulnerability and don't take it for granted. Also, don't be a judgmental jerk when sin is confessed to you (Galatians 6:1-2).

5. Pray. A lot. In person or virtually . . . whatever. Prayer is a way for us to speak the word of God over each other. Sometimes people will receive correction if you pray it instead of saying it. There's something different about telling a mentee, "Maybe you need to stop drinking every night." And praying, "God, would you help my friend to depend on you and turn to you first when she's feeling low." Make a list of people that you're discipling and regularly pray for them. Taking a mental note of their prayer requests when y'all get together (I write them down so I don't forget) will help you to gauge where they are at

spiritually. When you meet up, ask how they are doing regarding those prayer requests. Intercessory prayer is a huge part of discipleship. When we do this, we model being the holy priesthood of believers to one another (1 Peter 2:5) and imitate Jesus. If Jesus could ask his friends to pray with him when he was struggling, surely we can (Mark 14:32-40).

6. No Christianese. In seminary I did an assignment where I had to attend a worship service at a non-English-speaking church. It was more uncomfortable than I'd imagined it would be. Halfway through the service, I walked out because I had no idea what was going on. The next Sunday, I came back with my homie Pia, who is fluent in Spanish, and she whispered descriptions of what was happening throughout the service to me. Just like that, it felt like church. In the same way a language barrier was a stumbling block for me to be able to enter the life of that church and worship, Christian catch phrases and clichés can be an obstacle to understanding for people we're trying to share the good news with and mentor.

7. Contextualize your discipleship. Part of discipleship is creating an informal space to teach kinesthetic "we do" lessons—some more informal than others. If you're ministering or volunteering somewhere, invite your mentee to serve alongside you. Figure out how to get together with whoever you're discipling regularly and get creative. When I was a campus minister in Morningside Heights, I shared a closet-sized office with two other colleagues, and so I usually met outdoors with students I was mentoring, and we'd walk and talk. Only in NYC can a sidewalk

feel more private than a coffee shop. Most students didn't have lots of time to spare, so I tried to combine our meetings with activities they needed to do anyway. We'd grab coffee to-go and talk while walking near campus, grabbing a package from the campus mailroom, walking through Morningside Park, or shopping at Rite Aid (my errands) or Westside Market.

Little did I know, this rhythm of having mentoring meetings on the go, on the streets of NYC, would become a lifeline for the people I mentored and for me. When the Covid-19 pandemic shut NYC all the way down in the spring of 2020, and everything was outside and "to-go," I began meeting with mentees on park benches, on long walks down Eastern Parkway, and on my stoop. Walking and talking, listening, and wiping away tears, silently pleading with God for words to say and for discernment on when to be silent.

NYC exposes you. You're constantly surrounded by people. So when I'd be having a discipleship meeting and a homeless person interrupted my conversation to sell me something, or with a request for money or food, suddenly I was faced with an opportunity to embody Jesus' love, whether I wanted to or not. I can remember feeling annoyed that the reality of the pervasive poverty of my city kept "interrupting" my discipleship meetings. Then one day I realized that those moments were an answer to my *God, I can't see you. Show me where you're at work around me* prayers. They were an answer to my *God, please make yourself real to* [name of person I'm discipling] prayers because the best discipleship illustrates the kingdom principles that we're trying to teach.

Discipleship is holistic. It's about Christ being formed in us as we try to follow him in every area of life. Those "prayer and break bread" prayer walks I did with City Seminary of New York prepared me for these "interruptions," as I recalled that Jesus did ministry "on the way" and that he calls us to do the same in our cultural contexts. Our goal as disciples of Jesus is to proclaim the reign of this countercultural kingdom with our lives. If that's true, a good first step toward being in solidarity with the poor is to confront and resist the impulse to dehumanize the unhoused by avoiding (seeing and hearing) them so we can receive the blessing of our shared humanity. This is how Christ's heart is formed in us. Small acts of rejecting the status quo of our socioeconomically and racially stratified culture help us to press into the kingdom and proclaim to ourselves and others that another world is possible.

DISCIPLESHIP IS NOT ABOUT DROPPING KNOWLEDGE

In his book *Desiring the Kingdom*, philosopher James K. A. Smith says, "Being a disciple of Jesus isn't primarily a matter of getting the right ideas and doctrines and beliefs into your head in order to guarantee proper behavior; rather, it's a matter of being transformed into the kind of person who loves rightly—who loves God and neighbor and is oriented to the world by the primacy of that love."[3]

In other words, it's not what we know that forms us, it's what we love. As we make disciples, we're pouring out lives that have been (trans)formed by the Holy Spirit. No matter how long we've been in church, how many degrees we hold, or how long we've pastored or taught, as servants of Christ, we're entrusted with the mysteries God has revealed (Colossians 1:26). These mysteries aren't ours, and as servants, stewards, and shepherds

---

[3]James K. A. Smith, *Desiring the Kingdom: Worship, Worldview, and Cultural Formation* (Grand Rapids, MI: Baker Academic, 2009), 32-33.

of God's people, any wisdom we share has been freely revealed by the Spirit. So as we help others dig into the depths of the gospel, or help them understand how to exegete Scripture, we're just regifting what's been freely given.

A common goal of people I mentor is to grow in their prayer life. They say, "I want to pray better." And in that moment, I can be tempted to respond with behavior modification tactics, but what's more helpful is to ask what they think "pray better" means so I get an idea of how they view prayer. This usually leads to an honest confession. Sometimes they'll admit that they see prayer as a boring and useless chore, some say they hesitate to pray because they're racked with guilt and shame over sinful habits, and some have stopped praying altogether because unanswered prayer has made them doubt if God cares.

Asking good questions helps me not to waste time answering questions they aren't asking. My next step is to help them reframe how they view prayer. Drawing from *Desiring the Kingdom*, I explain how, if what we love is shaped by what we do, and if desire is shaped by our disciplines, then our prayer lives can form us like any other habit or ritual can form us.[4] I like to read Hebrews 4:14-16 together to show how Jesus (our high priest) offers up his life as a living sacrifice so that we can draw near to God in prayer, free of guilt and shame. Then I shimmy over to Romans 8:26, 34 where we learn that Jesus and the Holy Spirit intercede for us as we pray. I ask them how it makes them feel to know that God is praying for them (and not condemning them) as they pray. And then we talk some more.

In her book *Mentor for Life*, Natasha Sistrunk Robinson says, "Through mentoring we invite people to taste and see that the Lord is good. Once they have tasted, they must be taught how

---

[4]Smith, *Desiring the Kingdom*, 25.

to eat. They need to learn how to faithfully partake of his goodness and grace so they can continue to grow in faith."[5]

I try to help my spiritual siblings "learn how to eat" by reading through Scripture with them to reframe prayer as a shame-free zone of divine communion, conversation, and transformation, and not a boring task to be checked off. This isn't me facilitating behavior modification. Instead, I'm reminding them that prayer is an act of accepting God's invitation for us to come barefaced and with a bonnet on (naked and unafraid) into God's presence in the Spirit to "lay out the pieces of our life" (Psalm 5:3 MSG).

I explain that we don't pray just because it's what good Christians do but because prayer is a God-given means of grace that provides a context for us to draw near to God, offer up our worship, our tears, our laments, and allows the Holy Spirit to progressively transform our desires and affections. I explain that prayer proclaims to our hearts that we are dependent on and connected to God. It's coming to God not just to talk (conversation), but also to be with God (communion). Finally, it's also colaboring with God to accomplish the good works that God has prepared in advance for us to do. It's work in the Spirit. Then we read through John 17:20-26 because I figure it's a good idea to learn about prayer by reading through one of Jesus' prayers. We discuss how in this passage Jesus is praying for the restoration of what was lost in the garden on a global scale—the unfettered, unhindered access and communion between humanity and God. Jesus is praying that his followers would embody what he's about to die for. We talk about how prayer is a way to embody our union with Christ because sometimes this kingdom of God

---

[5]Natasha S. Robinson, *Mentor for Life: Finding Purpose through Intentional Discipleship* (Grand Rapids, MI: Zondervan, 2016), 45-46.

thing doesn't feel so real. Prayer is a tangible way for us to live into the union that Jesus died to make possible.

I currently spend a week of a group discipleship class at my church teaching on prayer. In that context, we discuss how the union and intimacy that Jesus prays for in John 17 can inform our prayer life. When we pray, we are an answer to Jesus' prayer that we would be brought "to complete unity" with the triune God (John 17:21). Many folks in the class who'd previously admitted to being incredibly bored with prayer were amazed by the notion that their humble act of prayer could be an answer to Jesus' recorded prayer in Scripture.

Finally, and most importantly, we pray together. Sometimes we sit in silent contemplative prayer and focus on a word or phrase in a text of Scripture. Sometimes we read Scripture out loud and allow what we've read to prompt our corporate prayer.

Jesus often taught by demonstration, so when I'm praying with someone that I'm discipling, I make it a point to honestly acknowledge my current struggles in my prayer so that they can experience a real person in real time that they respect, bringing their weaknesses to God without shame. I'm trying to exalt my need for God's grace and how the Holy Spirit works in my prayer life—not exalt my ability to pray.

Sometimes things are better "caught than taught," and sometimes hearing us include our struggles in prayer is all a person needs to be set free from the guilt and shame that makes them feel like God is sick and tired of hearing their prayers. In prayer and in life, discipleship entails a daily dying to self and setting our mind on things above (Colossians 3:2) as the Holy Spirit works to form the mind of Christ within us. Discipleship leads to a collaborative soul transformation, a metamorphosis wrought by the Spirit, without the cocoon to hide the ugly process. But somehow, it's still beautiful.

9

THE BEAUTY
OF DISCIPLESHIP

BINDING AND UNBINDING

A FEW YEARS AGO, while reading through John 11, I was struck by two things. Number one, Jesus is a great listener (more on this later). Number two is a little longer. In this passage, Jesus resurrects a man named Lazarus to new life in the presence of his disciples and "the many Jews" who are mourning with Lazarus's sisters. Jesus invites this crowd to experience his resurrection power, and after Jesus resurrects Lazarus, he commissions the onlookers to participate in the miracle and commands them to help Lazarus take off his grave clothes.

> So they took away the stone. Then Jesus looked up and said, "Father, I thank you that you have heard me. I knew that you always hear me, but I said this for the benefit of the people standing here, that they may believe that you sent me." When he had said this, Jesus called in a loud voice, "Lazarus, come out!" The dead man came out, his hands and feet wrapped with strips of linen, and a cloth around his face. Jesus said to them, "Take off the grave clothes and let him go." (John 11:41-44)

Lazarus had been buried for four days. He smelled. Despite this, Jesus invites the crowd to touch and unbind the resurrected Lazarus so their hearts could believe what their eyes saw. At the core, disciples are people who follow and learn from Jesus. This passage revealed to me that following Jesus is one part imitation of Christ and one part participation in the very real and miraculous work that Jesus is working through the Holy Spirit in people's lives. This revolutionized how I see discipleship in the local church.

Jesus' discipleship call is an invitation to participate with him in the project of the cosmic restoration of all things. "All things" includes me, you, and the most broken people we know. "All things" includes unjust systems and institutions of oppression. While working, Jesus says to his disciples, "Come and join me!" (Mark 8:6-7). In the group project of populating the kingdom of God, Jesus is the teacher who gives the assignment when he says, "Follow me and make disciples." Jesus is also "the smart one" in the group, as he empowers us to make disciples through the Holy Spirit. Jesus, who is our peace, reconciles all things to God (John 14:27) and re-creates peacemakers in his image (Matthew 5:9) to proclaim the good news of the gospel with our life and lips (Matthew 10:7).

Before his crucifixion, in an upper room with his disciples, Jesus taught that his disciples will be recognized by the world as we're tethered in love to one another (John 13:34-35). To put it plainly, in love Jesus binds himself, in love, to humanity so that we might be bound to one another and grow in Christlikeness together, empowered by the Spirit.

When my oldest son was in preschool, his teacher told us that whenever she taught a concept that involved physical activity and touch, he lit up and became laser focused. Similarly, when Jesus invites the crowd to unbind Lazarus from what is associated with death, Jesus teaches a kinesthetic "we do" discipleship lesson. Jesus' goal is that the mourners at Lazarus's funeral believe (John 11:4, 15, 40) that he has power to give new life, but also that they participate in the miracle as they unwrap Lazarus. It's not enough to watch Jesus weep, it's not enough to hear him pray and say, "Lazarus, come out!" Jesus invites the mourners to touch (and smell) Lazarus in response to their perceived doubt and experience a glimpse of the glory of God through Jesus Christ with all their senses. Jesus is always teaching (John 11:28), and the unbinding of Lazarus is an amazing "we do" lesson that ends with mourners being formed into believers who now know Jesus as the resurrection and the life in an experiential way for themselves. In the same way, Jesus calls "busy but bored" disciples to participate in the sanctifying work he is doing in people through mentoring, to fuel our faith. Jesus desires that his disciples follow him in an embodied way. If this makes you feel overwhelmed, remember discipleship is a group project that Jesus invites us to be a part of.

When my good friend Genevieve Smith preaches, she says it like this: "God wants us to be a part of restoring God's Beloved back to themselves. God wants us to be a part of a liberating work. And it requires that we unbind some people."[1]

Jesus invites anyone who has encountered the resurrection power of the Spirit to be united with other Spirit-filled people in their "newness of life" as we help one another unwrap from anything that is untrue of God and of ourselves. Whether it be helping people unwrap themselves from the principality of white supremacy, destructive addictions, sexism, or idolatry to political power—God calls us to help one another disentangle

---

[1] Genevieve Smith, "The Bread of Life: Luke 11:1-13," sermon preached on March 20, 2022, at Trinity Grace Church.

from what theologian Ekemini Uwan calls "additives to the faith that dim the beauty of the gospel."[2] As we walk alongside new believers we can help them "undress" from garments of death so they can "put on Christ" and walk in the abundance that God has re-created them for.

I imagine Lazarus was a little wobbly when he walked out of the grave. How do we practically walk alongside and mentor people who are learning how to walk and live into the resurrection life?

If the John 11 resurrection narrative seems fantastical and farfetched to you, that's because it is. Much of Jesus' ministry is coaxing belief in the impossible among his disciples and trying to get them to imagine that another way of living is possible (John 1:50; 3:12; Mark 9:24). Discipleship isn't mental assent to doctrine but following Jesus with all our senses, living in a way that reflects the culture of the kingdom of God. How do we encourage people to follow Jesus with all their senses? And what do we do when we get tired of encouraging?

WHEN DISCIPLERS DOUBT

It takes a sanctified imagination to accept Jesus' invitation to make disciples and join the Holy Spirit as we mentor, but this is how we experience the beauty of discipleship. To make disciples with joy, we must believe that God's plan—to populate a countercultural world that Jesus calls the kingdom—includes us and is bigger than we are. Then we can join God where he is already working. In John 20, a disciple named Thomas expresses doubt that Jesus is alive again. Some disciples tell Thomas they've seen the resurrected Christ, but Thomas is

---

[2]Ekemini Uwan, Christina Edmondson, and Michelle Higgins, *Truth's Table: Black Women's Musings on Life, Love, and Liberation* (New York: Convergent Books, 2022), 55.

traumatized by Jesus' violent crucifixion, and is *so* over having faith in what he can't see. And so, Jesus returns and asks Thomas to touch him where he was wounded. This is so that Thomas might believe in the miracle of resurrection and also believe in the healing that *could be* in light of the resurrection. Because if Jesus is truly resurrected, what isn't possible?

Jesus' conversation with Thomas reminds me of the dear believers I meet who have quit making disciples because of their own trauma-induced disappointment, doubt, or deconstruction. Maybe you can relate. Like Thomas, so many longtime Christians struggle with unbelief that has quenched any zeal to "make disciples," because what sense does it make to introduce people to a God that we're unsure about? What sense does it make to introduce people to a God that the people with whom we vehemently disagree about everything . . . worship? Thankfully, the Bible teaches us to "be merciful to those who doubt" (Jude 1:22), especially when that person is us. Then, and now, Jesus' response to the doubt of his disciples isn't anger, minimization, or disappointment, but instead an invitation for us to come closer to him. As we experience Jesus through his Spirit and his body, our souls are renewed (John 20:24-29).

Much of discipleship is following in Jesus' footsteps, becoming a safe place where people can honestly confess their doubts, confusion, and fear about God, and humbly walking with those people toward Jesus so that we can experience his mercy and grace. In our weakness, we walk toward Jesus with our own doubts and are formed to walk with someone else. What prepares your soul to walk in empathy with someone you're discipling is not a title or sense of certainty but the experience of wrestling with your own doubt while drawing close to the warm embrace of Jesus.

BINDING AND UNBINDING IN THE LOCAL CHURCH

As Westerners, we often think of salvation as an individual experience and discipleship as mostly about "how to apply the gospel to *my* life," or "how to get *my* blessing from God." But most of Jesus' teaching is addressed to communities, and the commands are meant to be worked out in community. Salvation is how the Holy Spirit gathers the people of God into this new humanity, and discipleship is how we live resurrection life together. I can't practice loving my neighbor alone. I can't bear someone's burdens unless I'm connected to a flesh-and-blood person.

And so how can this "binding and unbinding" work itself out in a local church? In the New Testament epistle to the church in Colossae, the apostle Paul uses the metaphor of "getting dressed" to describe discipleship in a community of Christ-followers. In Colossians 3:5-17, Paul encourages the Colossian Christians to "take off" and "put to death" anger, malice, lying, lust, and idolatry and then to "put on" (or cultivate) the virtues of Jesus because we can't be out here naked in the Spirit. I'm so glad Paul didn't end the letter exhorting the Colossians on what not to do because I meet a lot of people who believe that following Jesus is only about saying, "The things I used to do, I don't do no more!" Instead, it's also about how we embody the life of the one responsible for our new identity.

Paul teaches that disciples of Christ should "set their hearts and minds on things above, where Christ is" by deliberately living out the values of the kingdom of God:

> Therefore, as God's chosen people, holy and dearly loved, clothe yourselves with compassion, kindness, humility, gentleness and patience. Bear with each other and forgive one another if any of you has a grievance against someone.

Forgive as the Lord forgave you. And over all these virtues put on love, which binds them all together in perfect unity. (Colossians 3:12-14)

I don't think cultivating these virtues is easy or comes naturally, but I think "clothing ourselves" metaphorically means living in a way that reflects the reality of the kingdom of God as we're empowered by the Holy Spirit.

Metaphorically, we're not getting dressed alone. We can't. The commands in Colossians 3 are meant to be worked out in the lives of Spirit-filled people who are connected to other Spirit-filled people. "Putting on Christ" doesn't mean me trying to be more kind, compassionate, and humble on my own (my body getting dressed); it means cultivating these virtues in community (the body of Christ getting dressed). In Colossians 2:19, the apostle explains that the whole body of the church is "held together by" and "grows with a growth that is from God" (NRSV). This suggests that Spirit-birthed, Christlike virtues are what bind the body of Christ together in peace. Cultivating them in community is how we grow up into Christ.

But how does "getting dressed in Christ," or cultivating the compassion, kindness, humility, gentleness, patience, and love of Christ, help disciples of Christ make disciples of Christ in this hate-filled, racist, sexist, xenophobic, and wicked world? How do we live like Jesus when confronted with the reality that many people in the United States (some who even profess to be Christians) would be happy if many other Americans ceased to have basic civil rights, or ceased to exist at all?

Many times over the last few years as I've read Colossians 3, I've said out loud, "I don't want to put these clothes on." Metaphorically speaking, I'm too tired to get dressed or help anyone else get dressed. Extending kindness, humility, and compassion toward my perceived enemies seems foolish in the face of white supremacist domestic terrorism. It honestly has felt impossible to extend enduring lovingkindness to people who hate me and mine. And why is patience so difficult? Personally, as a Black woman in the United States, I'm tired of being patient and waiting for justice. And many of the Christians I mentor are also tired and struggle to embody the love of Jesus toward people who think saying "Black Lives Matter" is akin to communism.

When I was a child, I lost so many things. My bus pass, earrings, glasses, a Nintendo (don't ask). I remember digging through a pizzeria garbage can to retrieve my retainer, which I'd absentmindedly thrown away after eating a few slices. This was my second lost retainer, and my parents told me not to come home if I lost another one. But these days, it's not losing my retainer that I'm worried about—these days I'm tempted to lose my love. The lovelessness I described earlier in this book has threatened to invade my heart and soul. I'm tempted to lose my hope in God. And I know I'm not alone. The evil and wickedness of this present age has brought me to despair, rage, bitterness, or numbness, depending on the day.

In Proverbs 3:3 Solomon writes, "Let love and faithfulness never leave you: bind them around your neck, write them on the tablet of your heart." In Colossians 3:14, the apostle Paul writes that love is the epitome of all the Christlike virtues that God calls us to cultivate. And in those moments where I'm tempted to lose my love for people and to lose my hope in God, I need brothers and sisters in Christ to love me and bind love, patience, hope, and compassion around my neck so they're less easy to lose. We must surround ourselves with people who can help us get dressed in the virtues of Jesus. (Ideally, these are people you serve with at your local church or who live in your city.)

The Holy Spirit is the proof of God's promises to his people. When I doubt God's promises and my community reminds me that Jesus is the source of my love, they help me to grab hold of the love and grace of Jesus. This is the "fellowship of the Spirit" that the apostle Paul wrote about in 2 Corinthians 13:14. This kind of community points to and magnifies Jesus Christ. Empowered by the Spirit, Jesus fed the hungry, engaged people on the margins, and paid off people's debts (Matthew 17:27). Compassion is a major ingredient in the cross-shaped recipe of Jesus' life, and we reflect the glory of God and introduce people to Jesus when we embody the love and compassion that we ourselves receive from Jesus (Matthew 9:36; John 15:8). Every week, people muster up the courage to walk into church, but many times they're the walking wounded. People are broken and fragile and need to be reminded of the gentleness, kindness, and tenderheartedness of God toward them (Psalm 34:18). They need to be reminded that God doesn't want to beat them up and condemn them but desires to heal them.

Let us pray that the virtues of Christ would be formed in our communities (Galatians 4:19) so the church becomes a fully dressed community of disciples, bound together by the Spirit in peace, walking in the footsteps of our compassionate Savior.

COMPASSION VERSUS TOXIC POSITIVITY

When we are met with people's pain and trauma we can tend to minimize their pain (*It's not that bad, bro!*), over-spiritualize their pain (*This must be a demonic attack!*), or draw silver linings around their pain and respond with Christian clichés (*It could be worse, sis . . . but all things work together!*) because their pain is too painful for us to deal with. Entering the trauma of someone you're discipling can bring up your own trauma. I've fallen into the trap of meeting with a mentee, hearing them describe their frustration with the very real pain of life, and responding to their pain with a Christian cliché, or just trying to get them to cheer up. The sad thing is, if you know enough Scripture and have a way with words, you can do this well and never actually engage the pain and hurt someone is carrying.

Years ago, a campus ministry colleague pulled me to the side to tell me that a young woman I'd been mentoring had begun (secretly) meeting with her because the young woman felt I was "too happy" to bring her depression to. I was genuinely shocked because I really thought I was doing a great job mentoring this student. I saw she was a vibrant, caring student leader who was genuinely seeking after God. Thank God she had someone else to go to when she was being discipled poorly by me. And thank God my ministry colleague bore the fruit of gentleness, explained what was going on, and helped me learn how to "put on" compassion, instead of toxic positivity, going forward with future mentees.

Because my ministry partner corrected me in love many years ago, I'm much slower to speak, and when I do, I remind mentees of the power that God's grace is for them, that they are more than what they have done, that God wastes nothing—and sometimes I recognize that speaking might do more harm than good, and I just weep with them. This is the more patient and scenic route to discipleship, but in the words of the prophetess Mariah Carey, "love takes time." People are complex and trauma is nuanced, so embodying the compassion of Christ usually means slowing down, talking less, listening more, and entering their grief or pain or anxiety with care.

This isn't easy, but depending on the guidance of the Holy Spirit to enter people's pain and discern when to speak and when to shut up is what brings about spiritual maturity. Unseen spots are real. This is why having collaborative ministry teams in local churches made up of men and women (without hierarchy) is important. I'm grateful for Spirit-filled partners in ministry who have shown me the folly of using discipleship ministry as a means to "fixing people" in Jesus' name.

10

THE NECESSITY OF REST

IN 2012, I AND EVERY OTHER WOMAN I KNOW read the article, "Why Women Still Can't Have It All."[1] That summer, I was six months pregnant with our oldest child and working on an independent film in the sweet spot of Manhattan, where Soho, Chinatown, and Little Italy intersect. I spent my lunch breaks galivanting and devouring cannoli, tacos, banh mi, and pastries from the Chinese bakery. It was glorious. My group chats lit up with conversations about that article and how to realistically manage work, children, marriage, and everything else that life throws at us. Back then you couldn't tell me I couldn't have it all. Life comes at you fast.

"Another year, another fast." These are the words I wrote in my journal as I steeled myself for my church's annual week of fasting and prayer to bring in the new year in 2022. As much as I dislike fasting, it helps me to unplug from the firehose of media I consume, make room in my heart and mind to hear from God, and be present with myself and the people in my life.

[1] Anne-Marie Slaughter, "Why Women Still Can't Have It All," *The Atlantic*, July/August 2012, www.theatlantic.com/magazine/archive/2012/07/why-women-still-cant -have-it-all/309020.

Nine years after that glorious and naive summer of 2012, I'd just started my second year of working as the discipleship director at our church. I was feeling spiritually worn out. The discipleship class I taught was full of people who'd tell me how much the class was helping them grow spiritually. I was preparing to preach at our first in-person women's ministry gathering in two years as well as doing a lot of one-to-one mentoring at church. I'd just received a contract offer to write this book.

I was miserable.

And so, a few nights a week I'd have a beer, or two or three. Unfortunately, when you're on the other side of forty, you don't bounce back from a couple beers like you used to. I was more sluggish, had less patience with my children, and was generally awful to my husband. The sluggishness led to me trading off my morning devotional time for extra sleep and the next thing I knew I wasn't spending much time with God at all. I was stressed out, and I felt like I was losing my mind. My edges started edging off my scalp. There was so much unaddressed trauma that I'd been carrying after over a year and a half of trying to minister to everyone in my life during a pandemic.

I wrote "Lord, help me apply your truth to my trauma" in my journal and closed my eyes to try to pray. While praying, I vaguely remembered something my Anglican friend Kevin had mentioned years ago at a ministry conference (we all need Anglican friends), something about creating a "rule of life" to keep his sanity while juggling ministry and family life. So, I googled "rule of life" and the first thing that came up was a podcast called *The Eternal Current Podcast* with an episode on that topic.[2] I listened to an interview with Pastor

---

[2]"A Rule of Life (with Rich Villodas)," *The Eternal Current Podcast,* September 2019, https://open.spotify.com/episode/3Qk8iSBt8Dt8HZKOWH58hW?si=9324839 3c362410d.

Rich Villodas and Aaron Niequist. They explained that a rule of life is a reflective, contemplative tool of discernment to help people examine how they can lean into God. It sounded good to me, cuz I need to lean into something other than Knicks games and beer. After listening, I did some more googling and listened to a sermon by Pastor Rich, where he broke down this "rule of life" practice even further. It made so much sense.

In that sermon, titled "Examining Our Lives," Pastor Rich asked four questions:

1. What are the spiritual disciplines you need to anchor you in a life with God?"

2. What are the practices of self-care you need to care for your body and nurture your soul?

3. What core relationships do you need in this season of life to support you on a journey?

4. What are the gifts and passions within that God wants you to express for the blessing of others?[3]

These questions seemed helpful, so I decided to break with my Baptist upbringing and try this "rule of life" practice that apparently monks have been doing since the third century. Then I made a list with three categories: "Things that bring me delight," "Things that I need to limit or eliminate," and "Things that I have to do." Thank you, Pastor Rich.

The dope thing about writing things down is that it makes clear what feels fuzzy. My bootleg monastic assessment revealed that prayer, studying the Word, spending time with my husband, and playing with my children brought me delight,

---

[3]Pastor Rich Villodas, "Examining Our Lives," sermon, New Life Fellowship Church, December 26, 2021, https://youtu.be/6aAY7TByq0U.

but that's not what I was spending my time doing. I was spending time doom-scrolling on Twitter and reading news articles into the wee hours of the night, which made me angry and disillusioned. The angrier I got, the more I scrolled. My assessment also revealed that my forty-three-year-old body couldn't take my weeknight beer habit. I wrote in my journal, "Cut out weeknight beers. Social media is the key to my spiritual downfall. Check in with God the way I check Twitter. I miss my friends."

I confessed all of this to a good friend, made a commitment to carve out more time with my husband and my friends, go to sleep before 11:00 p.m., start jogging, commit to listening to an audio Bible podcast called *Get in the Word with Truth's Table*, find an affordable Black lady therapist, and decline any new speaking engagements for the year so I could finish writing this book without stressing my family out. Thanks to The Loveland Foundation,[4] I found an affordable, amazing "older" Black lady therapist who made me fill out a work-life balance worksheet to see where my life lacked balance, identify trouble spots, and set "balance goals." I desperately needed to make changes to balance prayer, rest, relationships, and work.

Talking with a therapist every week brought up a lot of memories from my childhood. As a child, my father made sure my brothers and I were immersed in Black history. I was Shirley Chisholm in my preschool play. "Black history is American history!" was something that my daddy would aggressively remind my brothers and me of while making us hot cereal in the morning. Missing school because I had the sniffles didn't happen much or ever, but just know that we were allowed to miss school to celebrate Black Solidarity Day.

---

[4]Learn more about the Loveland Foundation at thelovelandfoundation.org.

I spent every Fourth of July of my childhood at the International African Arts Festival in Brooklyn. After going to see Nelson Mandela speak at Boys & Girls High School in Bed-Stuy in 1990, my father gave me a book called *Kaffir Boy* by Mark Mathabane so we could learn more about the fight against the system of apartheid in South Africa. Basically, I am what my people call Blackity-Black. One weekend afternoon while watching *The Diary of Miss Jane Pittman*, I turned to my father and said, "Daddy, how come the slaves didn't just beat up and overthrow the slave masters? They worked so much! Shouldn't they have been stronger?" My father turned to me and said, "Rest makes you strong. Our enslaved ancestors were never allowed to rest. Their muscles never had time to heal and recover."

As a child I didn't understand that sleep deprivation was a form of torture that my ancestors had endured on the sugar plantations of Barbados. I didn't understand how being forced to constantly work and never being allowed to recover was a death sentence. To rest is to be human. How I rest (or don't rest) says so much about what I believe sustains me. After one of my therapy sessions, I realized that I had been working to "feed Jesus' sheep" without allowing Jesus to nourish me. Making disciples isn't easy. It's work in the Spirit. True ministry means bearing people's burdens and even though that's a blessing, it can make you weary. Ministry can also be a lonely place, especially as a woman. And out of a sense of wanting to "protect the sheep," ministers don't always share struggles and let people in church care for us.

After a few weeks of therapy, I realized that I needed Jesus to feed me before I could continue to feed anyone else. I had to commit to receive Jesus' invitation to rest in him—physically, emotionally, and spiritually. "Therefore go and make disciples of all nations," Jesus said, "baptizing them in the name of the Father and of the Son and of the Holy Spirit, and teaching them to obey everything I have commanded you. And surely I am with you always, to the very end of the age" (Matthew 28:19-20). Jesus also said, "Come to me, all you who are weary and burdened, and I will give you rest" (Matthew 11:28). As disciples who long to make disciples, how can we enter this rest when life doesn't stop? How can we obey Jesus' command to "make disciples" in a way that doesn't burn us out?

In the discipleship class that I teach at church, I reframe spiritual disciplines as a means of grace to enter the rest that Jesus invites his followers into (Matthew 11:28-30). As we process what it means to practically follow in Jesus' footsteps, I ask the class, how does Jesus describe discipleship? Inevitably someone says, "Don't you have to take up your cross and die to yourself to follow Jesus?" which elicits a combination of groans and cries of, "What part of being a Christian is fun?" because we conflate discipleship with cutting pleasure out of our lives and replacing fun with "Christian activities." To get my class off the ledge, I talk about Lauryn Hill.

At the 1999 Essence Awards, Lauryn Hill received an "Excellence Award" (Lauryn won everything that year). During her acceptance speech she said through tears, "I want to let young people know that it is not a burden to love [God] and to represent him and to be who you are, as fly and as hot and as whatever, and to still love God and to serve him. It's not a contradiction! It's not a contradiction."[5]

I remember listening to that speech and saying out loud to the television, "Really?! Serving God and following Jesus sure

---

[5]1999 Essence Awards, Speech, Lauryn Hill, www.youtube.com/watch?v=v_PPiUD 5GLA.

feels burdensome to me!" In hindsight, I think Lauryn was on to something. She intimately knew Jesus as someone who lifted burdens instead of piling them on, and that allowed her to describe discipleship like Jesus did. In the gospel narratives, Jesus describes new life in him as an "easy yoke" and a "light burden," and he invites his disciples to learn from him as we follow. "Take my yoke upon you and learn from me, for I am gentle and humble in heart, and you will find rest for your souls. For my yoke is easy and my burden is light" (Matthew 11:29-30).

In his book *The Spirit of the Disciplines,* Dallas Willard writes about how embodying the love of Jesus can't look like mustering up radical generosity or love or humility in on-the-spot situations. That doesn't work and it's not sustainable. He writes, "If we wish to follow Christ—and to walk in the easy yoke with him—we will have to accept his overall way of life as our way of life."[6] The kingdom of God that Jesus proclaims and embodies isn't a location; it's a way of life.

In my discipleship class, I ask, "How did Jesus rest? How did Jesus work? How did Jesus' love for people and his dependence on the Holy Spirit affect that balance?" Discipleship is imitation and participation, and when you think about it, Jesus had a dope work-life balance. Jesus' life wasn't all grocery miracles and exorcisms. Jesus got invited to weddings and turned up with friends and family! Jesus took naps (Matthew 8:24)! But Jesus also stole away from the crowds for private prayer (Matthew 14:23), and he did it so much that his followers often had to search for him (John 6:24). For me, ministry in these wilderness streets of NYC requires balance. Like Jesus, we all

[6]Dallas Willard, *The Spirit of the Disciplines: Understanding How God Changes Lives* (New York, NY: HarperOne, 1988), 8.

need times of worshipful solitude where we can contemplate the beauty of God, pray for grace, repent, cast our burdens down, and allow the Spirit to transform our desires. But we also need to study the Bible, pray, worship, celebrate, and serve in community. Over time, as we seek to depend, rest, and love like Jesus, motivated by desires that are shaped by the Spirit, our interior devotional life and communal life will look more like Jesus' own.

One of the Scriptures that I clung to during that new year's fast was 1 Kings 19, a narrative about the prophet Elijah. Elijah is on the run in the wilderness because the monarchy is trying to kill him for being God's mouthpiece. Afraid and oppressed by the heaviness of the prophetic call on his life, he sits down under a broom tree and prays to die (1 Kings 19:3-4). God's response to his suicidal prayer is to feed him and put him to sleep. Elijah wakes up, sees the food waiting for him, and a voice says, "Get up and eat, for the journey is too much for you" (1 Kings 19:7). It was so comforting to be reminded that God knows our limitations and is pleased with our dependence. What a gift to be reminded that God sustains his servants in his presence and that rest is holy and sacred to God. Isn't it wild how from the Old Testament to the New, the Bible is consistent on how sometimes the most spiritually healthy thing we can do is take a nap?

And our spiritual formation doesn't always have to be in church! Prayer while taking a walk or a bike ride or buying groceries can be a place where your burdens are lifted, and you're renewed and formed to make disciples. Prayer is a very real way to imitate Jesus and to participate in what God is doing in the world. But intercessory prayer (praying to God on someone's behalf) is also a way to rest as we listen for God's voice and direction! For example, when tragedy strikes the life of someone I'm mentoring, and they share their pain and anger toward God with me, I can feel anxiety and a pressure to sustain their faith and give them credible reasons why they shouldn't turn away from God because of that tragedy. In that moment, intercessory prayer is a way to give my anxiety about them and their situation to God and to rest in God's power and sovereignty over their spiritual walk. Like the apostle Paul says, we must "press on" to know Jesus to become like him (Philippians 3:10-14), but the press is also rest! Do we see prayer as rest? Or do we see it as a holy colaboring with God so that our souls can rest? Maybe it's both.

Our limitations are a good thing. In the words of New Testament professor Beth Felker Jones, "Finitude is a gift. It reminds us that we're not God. It teaches us to trust in the One who is infinite, and it teaches us how to love the finite things we get the finite time to love."[7] Our limitations bring us to the end of ourselves and to the ever-flowing fountain of God's grace and mercy that we need to follow Jesus. I think being at peace with our limitations is what Jesus wanted his disciples to understand when he said, "Learn from me." He was one hundred precent God, but he leaned into the limitations of his incarnation to show us how to depend on God and truly be human (Philippians 2:6-7). The more we accept this truth, the easier the yoke and the lighter the burden because it reminds us that we're not God.

Viewing sabbath rest either as a burden or as a blessing reveals what we believe about God. Capitalism thrives on people sacrificing their bodies, souls, and minds on the altar of productivity. And it's demonic. I live in NYC, which is where many

---

[7]Beth Felker Jones, "I Don't Know How She Does It," Church Blogmatics, May 11, 2023, https://bethfelkerjones.substack.com/p/i-dont-know-how-she-does-it.

people come to "make it." If I had a dollar for every college student who used to tell me, "I don't know what to do when I have nothing to do," I'd be rich. When working in campus ministry, I'd have meetings with students who felt real guilt for "not doing enough" even though they were taking seventeen credits, had two internships, and were on the executive board for multiple clubs.

To address this workaholic mindset, I regularly read through Amos 8:4-6 with mentees and discuss how the prophet prophesied that God would judge Israel's ruling elite for "trampling the needy" and showing contempt for God's Sabbath because the Sabbath was bad for business. Then, and now, the world doesn't want us to rest (in Jesus, in prayer, in solitude, or in our beds). And at times we're our worst enemies because we convince ourselves that more work equals a better us. Capitalism is a principality, and the devil is a liar. But alas, I too forget to practice what I preach.

After I had my lil nervous breakdown, therapy helped me to see that I'd fallen into the rut of seeking God to prepare Bible studies, curriculum, and sermons, but not to be with God and rest in his presence. I'd be reading the Scriptures and God would reveal something and I'd be like *Oooh, this would make a dope application in my discipleship class!* before applying that revelation about God to my life. It was so focused on using the Word of God as a tool to disciple others that I forgot that it was a resting place for me. I was busy working for God, but missing out on experiencing God because I forgot that God's Word is a refuge.

Therapy also helped me see that my breakneck pace of life was a huge obstacle to my own discipleship and spiritual health. Time spent in private worship was rest that prepared Jesus for ministry, and the same is true for us. If we're discipling people and relying on grit, charisma, intellect, and spiritual gifts, Jesus' discipleship calling will be too heavy. We won't be able to bear the weight. If seeking God is not a lifestyle, the patience, compassion, love, and generosity that we're called to embody when making disciples will feel like a heavy burden instead of the abundant life that Jesus promises.

These days, sabbath looks like not working myself to death (in the name of ministry) but taking time to play with my sons and call my parents so I can hear them tell me about things like what somebody's grandbaby did, what's on sale at Key Food, an interesting article they read, or a story that I've already heard a thousand times. It looks like taking time to call my friends and talk about whatever, or cooking a really good meal and then eating it without scrolling through Twitter to see who the main character of the day is. It looks like taking a long walk around the park after dark with my husband. In the Old Testament Scriptures, rest is a reward and a command. Under the new covenant of the Spirit, we are invited by God to rest in Jesus so that he can form us to love like he does as we try to help people follow Jesus in everyday life.

11

HOW TO WALK IN THE WILDERNESS

WHEN I WORKED IN CAMPUS MINISTRY, my favorite (and most challenging) Bible study to teach was the book of Hebrews. It was challenging because most of the students were unfamiliar with the Old Testament passages that the author of Hebrews quotes heavily from. But it was my favorite because of how practical it was.

In Hebrews 3:7-4:16, the author quotes Psalm 95 (which recounts Exodus 15–17 and Numbers 13–14) to compare the "wilderness journeys" of the original audience of Hebrews to their ancestors who were stuck between bondage and glory. Their ancestors had been freed from slavery to Pharaoh but in the wilderness, they fell into idolatry (they were melting earrings, y'all) and lovelessness (they plotted to kill Moses, y'all)—a.k.a. the twin kryptonite to discipleship. Fresh out of the Red Sea, the Israelites complain about a lack of drinkable water to Moses, and God provides water. Problem solved, right? No.

A little while later, they get hungry and start reminiscing for the "meats of Egypt" and accuse Moses of rescuing them only to let them starve to death. Once again, God provides—this time with quail and manna (Exodus 16). But the next time they complain, Moses doesn't let it go and asks the people two questions: "Why do you quarrel with me?" and "Why do you put the LORD to the test?" (Exodus 17:2). In Exodus 15–17, their beef with Moses reveals a deeper distrust of God, despite God's faithfulness to provide sustenance after delivering them from bondage. Throughout the wilderness journey to the Promised Land, the people cycle through anxiety that God won't provide, fear that God has abandoned them, resentment toward God and Moses, and then . . . God provides what they need.

Like the children of Israel, as a disciple of Jesus who makes disciples, you will have moments when you doubt God's presence and provision and ask yourself, "Is God with me?" That happens to me when someone I'm mentoring shares something heavy with me and then stops communicating. No texts, no phone calls, nothing. That's the wilderness to me. In that moment, all I want to do is comfort them, pray with them, encourage them, and share the promises of God. But I can't make them communicate with me. In those moments, I wonder, *Am I in the right line of work? Is God really with me? Maybe I should go back to working in television and film.* And then I pray. I tell God what I wish I could say to them. In those moments, even though I'm aware of my limitations, I try and remember God's power. In these moments, I'm reminded that making disciples is a holy collaboration and I'm not working alone. Because as I pray and wait, I'm forced to rest from my striving and trust that God is working (much harder than I) in the Spirit.

How do we resist the temptation to idolatry and lovelessness as we seek to make disciples? For us, the "wilderness" is wherever we feel abandoned or shortchanged by God. As you seek to make disciples in this broken world, like Moses, prepare to be misunderstood, prepare to feel inadequate, and prepare to feel abandoned by God. Whether you're trying to make disciples at your church or disciples of your children (or both), prepare to be angry with God and, like Moses, ask, "What am I to do with these people?"

As I taught through Hebrews with the college students, we saw ourselves in the Scriptures that described the in-between of the wilderness. One morning I was talking with someone I was discipling who'd been struggling with controlling their anger. When I suggested that we pray about it, they said, "You've been praying for me for a year, and nothing has changed! What's the point?" I took a deep breath, nodded silently, and we began to pray together—but I can't front: as we prayed, I wondered if they were right. Israel's cyclical behavioral pattern of crisis, unbelief, disappointment (with God), and then blessing or chastisement felt very familiar.

When quoting Psalm 95 in Hebrews 3:7-11, the author of Hebrews doesn't say "as the psalmist says," but attributes authorship to the Holy Spirit who inspired those words: "So, as the Holy Spirit says: 'Today, if you hear his voice, do not harden your hearts as you did in the rebellion, during the time of testing in the wilderness'" (Hebrews 3:7-8). And since the Holy Spirit is the same yesterday, today, and forever, this word is for us as well. Then, and now, Hebrews 3:7–4:13 helps disciple-makers locate our story in God's redemptive story. We've been saved by God from bondage to sin but still struggle and strive in the "in-between" of the wilderness as we press toward the goal of our salvation.

For some of the college students I ministered to, failing organic chemistry and then feeling worthless because they had to switch majors, felt like the wilderness. Being forced to choose between a monthly MetroCard or eating because the financial aid department made a "mistake" felt like the wilderness.

Struggling with suicidal ideations because they got a C on a test and didn't know who they were anymore felt like the wilderness. Pumping breastmilk between discipleship meetings and wondering if I was in over my head felt like the wilderness. College was a place where students' belief in God was constantly being tested, and, as I tried to make disciples out of them, so was mine.

While teaching through Hebrews, my goal was to reframe spiritual disciplines like fasting, solitude, prayer, and meditating on God's Word to become means of rest and not burdensome Christian tasks to be checked off. Reading through these "wilderness journey" Scriptures revealed how life can make us doubt God's Word, God's love for us, and God's power. As a class, we also realized that being alone in the wilderness was a bad look. And so I began to ask the students and myself, "Who is with you in the wilderness? Who is helping you to hear God's voice and respond in faith and obedience? Who is encouraging you to draw near to God, to keep your heart soft in the wilderness?"

Genuine faith perseveres, but community strengthens our ability to persevere. The author of Hebrews says, "See to it, brothers and sisters, that none of you has a sinful, unbelieving heart that turns away from the living God. But encourage one another daily, as long as it is called 'Today,' so that none of you may be hardened by sin's deceitfulness" (Hebrews 3:12-13). Even when life is tough, we can resist the urge to fake it, let our guard down, and "rest" around people who love us, striving toward the "upward call" alongside one another. We need people to help us hold on to God's unchanging hand when we want to let go. We need people to remind us that God is the shade on our right hand—that shade doesn't take away the heat but makes it bearable.

I love how the author of Hebrews exhorts the reader three times in this passage that discipleship is a group project:

> Let us draw near to God with a sincere heart and with the full assurance that faith brings, having our hearts sprinkled to cleanse us from a guilty conscience and having our bodies washed with pure water. Let us hold unswervingly to the hope we profess, for he who promised is faithful. And let us consider how we may spur one another on toward love and good deeds, not giving up meeting together, as some are in the habit of doing, but encouraging one another—and all the more as you see the Day approaching. (Hebrews 10:22-25)

Since taking a vacation isn't always an option, drawing near to God to pray with people is a very affordable way to enter rest. God will bear our burdens, but so can flesh-and-blood people if we humble ourselves and let them. Sometimes I want to let go of God, but I'm grateful when I rest in the encouragement of a friend who reminds me that Jesus is holding all things (including me) together. Being present with God gives me strength to be present in community, and as we make disciples, both are essential to our spiritual formation. Drawing near to God creates a space for God to grow our love for people and help us to see them like God does.

Reminding myself of this every day helps me not to die in the wilderness seasons of ministry as I try to muster up love for people out of the shallow wells of my own grit. In my own strength, I can't love people or trust God like the Word calls me to, and if I try, I'll end up resenting the people I'm trying to make disciples of. But drawing near to God and then people (in that order) softens my heart to receive God's promises by faith so that I can encourage someone else to do the same.

One particular morning as I rode the subway to campus, going over my Bible study notes on Hebrews 10, with my breastmilk pump bag resting near my legs, I read this passage: "Therefore, brothers and sisters, since we have confidence to enter the Most Holy Place by the blood of Jesus, by a new and living way opened for us through the curtain, that is, his body, and since we have a great priest over the house of God, let us draw near to God" (Hebrews 10:19-22). At that moment, the 3 train became a makeshift tabernacle for me to confess my exhaustion, confusion, and self-doubt to God—free from shame—and I was filled with fresh gratitude for Jesus.

Making disciples will drive you to your knees or it will drive you out of the faith. Making disciples is beautiful but it's work in the Spirit and it's not easy. After a while, the grit and the giftings will only take you so far. When I was a kid, I loved playing video games and I specifically remember the anxiety and fear that I would feel when my character's "power" got low. I also vividly remember the freedom, confidence, and security that I felt when my character would get a "new life" or have its "power" renewed because it jumped onto a magic mushroom (Super Mario Brothers) or ate a piece of fruit (Pac-Man). In the same way, as we journey through the wilderness of life seeking to make disciples, we need to get "powered up" by coming to God daily to receive the grace, mercy, and necessary rest that God supplies.

WALK LIKE JESUS IN THE WILDERNESS

If you take Jesus' command to make disciples seriously, there will be times when you wonder if what you're doing is helpful. As of this writing in 2023, there have been 484 mass shootings in the United States.[1] Disciple-making in these times will make you question if what you're telling people about God's power, presence, and provision is true.

In these moments, Jesus isn't only the source of our hope and rest; in his humanity, Jesus also models how to have faith, persevere, and resist idolatry and lovelessness in a deeply broken world. Moses and Jesus were both tasked with leading God's people into freedom and rest, but only Jesus finished the journey victorious over sin and death. Unlike Moses and Aaron (Israelite priests) who were denied entry into the Promised Land because of their sin, Jesus (our great high priest) has passed through the wilderness of this world, entered the land of rest, and finished our redemption.

Hebrews 2:17 says, "He had to be made like them, fully human in every way, in order that he might become a merciful and faithful high priest in service to God." God does through Jesus what he previously intended to achieve through humanity. Jesus has already obediently walked the path that we are supposed to walk. With Jesus as our genuinely human forerunner, we can respond to trials with faith and follow the same pattern of life that he embodied, especially when we're confused, weary, or doubt that God cares. Jesus is intimately acquainted with suffering in the wilderness and can sympathize with our wilderness weakness (Hebrews 2:18). Jesus knows that in the wilderness, we're tempted to disobey God's Word, we struggle with unbelief, and we become prone to being deceived by sin. Jesus knows that the wilderness can make you blind to the action of God. But Jesus says, "Take my yoke and learn from me"

---

[1]Kiara Alfonseca, "There Have Been More Mass Shootings Than Days in 2023, Database Shows," ABC News, October 26, 2023, https://abcnews.go.com/US/mass-shootings-days-2023-database-shows/story?id=96609874.

(Matthew 11:29), so let's look to Jesus and learn from him how to walk in the wilderness.

When Jesus is baptized with water and the Spirit, Jesus fulfills the words spoken through the prophet Isaiah. The glory of the goodness of God is revealed as Jesus is affirmed and commissioned for ministry by his Father. Jesus tells John that he must be baptized so that "all righteousness" would be fulfilled. Theologians have written that the Father's words of affirmation come from Genesis 22:2, Isaiah 42:1, and Psalm 2:7 to show that the Law, the writings, and the Prophets are fulfilled in Jesus.[2] When Jesus is baptized, the audible voice of God the Father is a clue to all present that Jesus' mission is messianic and the fulfillment of the story of Israel. Jesus is part of a much bigger story.

As we seek to live out our discipleship calling in this modern-day wilderness, it's life-giving to be reminded that our re-creation in Christ is part of a much larger story, that we're empowered by the Spirit, and that our work has eternal significance. Like a child at the playground attempting to go on the "big slide" who occasionally looks back to a grownup for assurance, we must look to God every day—and not people or titles—to be reminded of the power and sovereignty of the one who calls us—especially when we're weary. We become like what we behold and as we look to Jesus, who, what, and how we love is formed by the Spirit. Little by little. The same Holy Spirit that descended and rested on Jesus at his baptism is freely given to anyone who is united with Christ by faith, to empower us to be on mission with God. Life can make us question God's promises, and when it does, knowing that our discipleship calling is part of God's cosmic plan of redemption helps me to hold on.

---

[2] Vern S. Poythress, *The Shadow of Christ in the Law of Moses* (Phillipsburg, NJ: Presbyterian and Reformed, 1991), 254.

The same Spirit that descended on Jesus at his baptism led him into the wilderness, and helped Jesus persevere when he was tested there. Jesus' journey into the wilderness provides a "perseverance pattern" for weary disciples like you and me. If you have an older sibling, you know how helpful it is to have someone go before you—conquer middle school, ride a bike, and go to college before you—so you believe you can do those things too. As we make disciples and follow in the footsteps of Jesus, our older brother who has gone before us, it's reassuring to know that just because life feels like the wilderness doesn't mean I'm out of God's will. The same Spirit who empowered Jesus to teach with power and cast out demons led him into the wilderness to be tempted. In the wilderness, the tempter whispers to Jesus, "If you are the Son of God, tell these stones to become bread" (Matthew 4:3), and the Holy Spirit reminds Jesus of a promise from Deuteronomy 8:3. Jesus says, "It is written: 'Man shall not live on bread alone, but on every word that comes from the mouth of God'" (Matthew 4:4).

DISCIPLES ARE SUSTAINED BY THE WORD

When Jesus speaks these words to the tempter, he embodies trust in the Father. Jesus is at the end of his fast and doesn't deny that he is in need. Jesus doesn't deny his physical hunger and thirst, and he doesn't hold God in contempt for the conditions of the wilderness. When Satan tempts Jesus to doubt his identity with the words, "If you are," unlike the Israelites in the wilderness, Jesus leans into the limitations of his humanity and humbly depends on the affirming words of his Father, the power of the Holy Spirit, and the Hebrew Scriptures that he learned as a child. In the wilderness, the "living bread" got hungry and was sustained by the Word. As he persevered in the wilderness, Jesus identified with every one of us who has ever suffered and wondered if God was there.

Jesus is subjected to demonic temptation that is eerily similar to the mocking that he would endure during his crucifixion: "Come down from the cross, *if you are* the Son of God!" (Matthew 27:40). On the cross and in the wilderness, the living Word fought the lies of the enemy and was sustained by the Old Testament Scriptures. Jesus knew his identity, value, and worth weren't wrapped up in the perception of the enemy but in the will of God the Father. Empowered by the Spirit, Jesus didn't just say, "man shall not live by bread alone." Jesus *lived* "man shall not live by bread alone" (Matthew 4:4).

I don't know what the demons in your city sound like, but in NYC, they whisper things like, *You are what do! You are what you have! You're worthless if you're unemployed! You are what you produce! If you're not making money, who are you? You are what school your child gets into! You are your LSAT score!* And so, I encourage people I mentor to follow Jesus' example of fighting the lies of the enemy with God's Word so they can remind themselves of who they truly are and so God can reveal himself to them as a sustainer. In John 15:7-8, Jesus teaches that as we abide in him, and as his words abide in us, we can ask whatever we wish, and it will be done for us. There's something about God's Word being alive and at work in us (abiding) that will help us to refute demonic lies like Jesus did in the wilderness. For example, when reading the Gospels, we discuss how when Jesus called fishermen to himself to "make them fishers of men," he was affirming that that they were more than their job or paycheck. We fight Satan's lies when we let God's Word remind us that we have dignity, value, and worth just because we're created the image of God. Period.

Jesus didn't have Scripture memorized to impress people. The Hebrew Scriptures had formed him. Like his prophetic predecessor Ezekiel (see Ezekiel 3:2-3), Jesus "ate" the Word, and it strengthened him when he was weary, hungry, and tempted. Christians love to tell other Christians to memorize Scripture and call that discipleship. We have memorization competitions and everything! But if I read Matthew 4 with someone I'm discipling and tell them, "Fight temptation by memorizing Scripture so you can be like Jesus," that may or may not work. Instead, I ask people I disciple questions like these:

- When life makes you doubt who God says you are, does Scripture help you remember?
- What does that Scripture passage reveal to you about God's character and provision?
- How does God's Word sustain you?
- When is the last time the Word of God caused you to love someone or yourself more deeply?

As we look at Jesus' time in the wilderness, let's ask ourselves: What's our relationship like with the Word of God? How has the Word of God sustained us in the sometimes wilderness of disciple-making? How does God's Word form your relationship with yourself? If the Word of God doesn't form Christ in us and help us to obey God and love people, who cares how much we memorize? If we don't depend on God, we will eventually depend on something else.

Jesus' temptation in the wilderness also reveals the importance of having the Word "stored up" in our hearts (Psalm 119:11). If the Holy Spirit's job is to remind us of the words of Jesus, it helps to have the Word of Jesus in our hearts to give Holy Spirit material to work with. I learned how to play the saxophone in the sixth grade. I hated practicing my scales, but knowing my scales helped me to improvise when the leader of my high school jazz band called my name for a solo. In the same way, when we read the Bible and allow the Word to penetrate our hearts, and when someone we're discipling calls us with a crisis (or when shit hits the fan in our own lives), the Holy Spirit has chapter after chapter of God's Word to work with and apply to that person's situation as we seek to encourage them.

Resting in the promises of God, empowered by the Spirit, Jesus is sustained in the wilderness by the Word, and he lives forever to sustain all things by his word (Hebrews 1:3). Remember, "all things" includes you and me. Bearing fruit is not about working harder or following Jesus better. It's about being fed by Jesus and being pruned by God, which produces love, joy, peace, and patience in our lives. Tree branches don't work hard, they just receive life from the source. Our relationship with Jesus and the power of the Holy Spirit is what provides the fuel for us to make disciples and have joy doing it (1 John 4:13). The Word of God is alive (Hebrews 4:12) and we need the living Word to form our hearts to follow Jesus. As we let God's Word become at home within us and form our hearts, our prayers can be "others focused" without us resenting the people that we pray for because of the overflow of grace that the Word produces. Does the God's Word feel at home in your heart? Or does it feel like a guest? When I'm at the home of a good friend, I don't need to ask for directions or permission to find things-because of the many times that they've said, "Make yourself at home" to me. My prayer is that God's Word would feel so at home in our hearts that it would go where it needs to without having to ask permission—to give peace to our minds and comfort our souls. Amen.

12

WHERE'S THE FRUIT? TRUST THE HOLY GHOST

WHILE WORKING IN CAMPUS MINISTRY, my time was largely spent teaching weekly Bible studies and chatting with students in one-on-one meetings over countless cups of coffee. In our initial discipleship meetings, some students told me they'd grown up attending church but never really enjoyed it. Some told me that they only came to my Bible study so they could tell their parents they were doing "something Christian." Others told me that everything they knew about God was what their parents taught them. No matter how our initial conversations began, most would end with some variation of, "But I'm trying to figure out Jesus and what I believe for myself." These students looked up to me because I was a source of biblical and life wisdom for them, and I wasn't too corny (or so they said). And I was excited to get to the "teaching them to obey everything I have commanded you" part of discipleship with them.

I distinctly remember a conversation that I had with a student we'll call Chloe. She was in her junior year and had joined the Bible study midway through the semester. When I asked if she had any Christian friends, she told me that she'd tried to hang out with some Christians on campus but never felt like she fit in because they presented as "perfect" and never admitted to struggling with sin. This discouraged her from being open with her own struggles for fear of being judged. She was racked with guilt and shame and felt like she had nowhere to turn. She even felt too guilty to pray. And so, in my tiny office, I began to open up to her about my journey from being a promiscuous pothead who sang in the gospel choir in college (the organist sold weed), to being reintroduced to Jesus while interning in Los Angeles, to struggling to understand the meaning of grace as a young Christian—I would proclaim fasts in order to "get rid of sinful desires." (Don't do that, by the way. You'll just end up hungry and legalistic.)

We joked about how God must have a sense of humor because here I was teaching weekly Bible studies to college students when I was that girl in college smoking weed out of a dollar bill. As we spoke, I reminded her that Jesus didn't come for people who have it all together but for "sinners" (Matthew 9:12-13), and that the same Holy Spirit that guided and empowered me dwelled inside of her. After we talked and prayed together, Chloe said, "You seem so normal, and you make following Jesus seem possible. I want to commit to your Bible study."

The wild thing is that what drew her to the Bible study (where she was able to connect with relatable Christians) wasn't my exegetical skill or pious lifestyle. My willingness to exalt the power of God's grace in my life as opposed to deepness, grit, or self-discipline was a reminder that she and I weren't as different as she'd thought, and that the Holy Spirit was alive in her as well. That conversation and many others like it shaped how I view discipleship and mentoring. One of the easiest ways to reflect the character of Christ is to be vulnerable and transparent—not for shock value, but for the sake of others. If people are going to be drawn to something, let them be drawn by the beauty of God's grace, our gratitude for grace, and the power of the gospel.

One last thing: Chloe was a young woman of African descent who grew up being "the only Black person" in predominately White Christian spaces in her hometown. She shared that my being comfortable in my own skin as a Black woman made her feel like she belonged in the body of Christ as a Black woman. I'm so glad she hadn't met me when I was trying to teach and sound like John Piper or Tim Keller. It had taken years for me to stop trying to teach like some famous pastor or Bible teacher, but I did (thank you, Jesus), and she noticed. No matter what your race or ethnicity, there's someone who needs to see Jesus embodied in you with all your quirks and idiosyncrasies—just the way that you are. Whether you were raised in a big urban city, the suburbs, or a rural town, be yourself and let the Holy Spirit shine through you. Resist the temptation to present as something that you're not, and let people see the ongoing work of Jesus in your life.

Chloe opened up to me, and my response was informed by my relationship with God's grace. However, many of the people I train as discipleship leaders struggle with responding to confessed sin. Too often, "discipleship accountability groups" are places where sin is belittled or where people are condemned and end up feeling like hopeless sinners or pious liars. No one wants to be a judgmental jerk, but how can we seek to be agents of gentle restoration (see Galatians 6:1) when people share destructive patterns of sin with us? How do we take seriously Jesus' command to love our neighbor and to extend the same grace that we freely receive? Being partakers of grace informs how we respond to confessed sin. We can remind a spiritual sibling that the mercies and steadfast love of God never run out, no matter what they've done (Lamentations 3:22-23). We can also remind them that the gospel frees us to resist being defensive about and rationalizing our favorite sins so that we can receive God's grace. Being partakers of grace helps us to respond to confessed sin with the same grace and truth that Jesus Christ offers to us (John 1:17).

I'll never forget hearing Dr. Christina Edmondson say, "We only extend the grace that we think we need,"[1] and mature Christians know that we need an eternal amount. If God's lovingkindness is what leads us to repentance, then responding to confessed sin with spiritualized threats or behavior modification tactics is problematic. I recently led a discipleship training class at my church, and during the Q&A a young man said, "I've been taught that we can love people to hell. How do we approach people that need to feel conviction?" I said to him, "We can't make anyone feel conviction. Pray for people. Talk to God about them and let God work!" The Word of God is the Holy Spirit's sword, not ours. Weaponizing the Scriptures to shame people is bullying, not mentoring. Being led by the Spirit informs how I respond to confessed sin because as I remember that the Holy Spirit is progressively perfecting me day by day, I'm more apt to remind my spiritual siblings that they too are being perfected by the Spirit and not the flesh. Bearing one another's burdens in this way is how we imitate Christ (Galatians 6:2) and mediate the blessings of the gospel in a practical way.

I recall talking to some college students about the boundless love of Christ and praying for that love to permeate the campus

---

[1]Christina Edmondson, "The Gospel for the Sinner," Legacy Disciple Conference, August 20, 2019, www.youtube.com/watch?v=gl2sVDgTfuw&t=128s.

and a student said, "I don't love anybody that much! I don't have it in me!" I appreciated her honesty. If we're engaged in making disciples, we will have seasons where we feel too depleted to minister to anyone else. And there's nothing wrong with that. As I mentioned earlier, Christians should be the first people to embrace sabbath rest as God's gift because rest reflects what we believe about God's goodness and the power of the Holy Spirit working in and around us.

If you've lived long enough, you know that there will be seasons of suffering where we're less busy but still must show up in people's lives. Making disciples is beautiful, but discipleship is a lifelong journey and life can be difficult and messy. Ministry has taken me to psychiatric wards to pray with someone in my Bible study who unsuccessfully tried to end their life. It's also taken me to the 911 dispatch to report the location of a friend who was experiencing suicidal thoughts. But discipleship has also taken me to the throne of grace as I wept tears of joy with a student who experienced God's grace and love for the first time and felt like they'd been reborn. When the Holy Spirit regenerates people's hearts, eternity begins.

As the Spirit works in people's hearts, we partner with the Spirit as we serve, love, and help people grow in spiritual maturity. It's a holy collaboration. As I mentored those college students, my greatest joy was watching them grow in spiritual maturity and begin to minister to each other apart from me. While prepping to teach a Bible study on Philippians with my students, I learned that about ten years had passed between the birth of the community of Christ-followers in Philippi and when Paul wrote what we know as the letter to the Philippians.[2]

---

[2]Blue Letter Bible, "Timeline of the Apostle Paul," www.blueletterbible.org/study/paul/timeline.cfm.

That reminded me that spiritual growth takes time and patience. Don't be discouraged when mentees don't grow as fast as you want them to. Trust the Spirit to do the work!

Most of my ministry experience has been serving adolescents and young adults, and though this demographic can be more teachable than their older Christian counterparts, they can be flaky and struggle with the mundane and everyday ordinariness of the Christian life. No matter how interactive and exciting I tried to make our Bible studies, the students that I taught regularly complained that the Bible was boring and irrelevant to their lives. They would fall asleep *in my face* in the middle of my Bible study. They would agree to discipleship meetings and then hit me with a "my bad, I overslept" text after I'd been waiting for an hour. And if the love of Christ wasn't my fuel for ministry?? BAYBEEEE I might have cussed one of them out, or even worse, I might have gone through the motions of ministry all the while growing bitter and resentful.

I remember one night in my first year of campus ministry, coming home from campus feeling so depressed because a group of students weren't showing up to my weekly Bible study even though I knew they were struggling emotionally. As I moped, I imagined the hypothetical awful decisions that they would make because they wouldn't listen to my admonitions to prioritize God in their busy schedules. Then as I began to complain to my husband, he listened and then gently reminded me that I wasn't the Holy Spirit.

My sadness came from the love I had for them, but over time I began to subconsciously equate their spiritual growth with my fitness as a minister. If they weren't growing, it was my fault. So toxic! As I talked to my mentors, they helped me realize that the four-year intervals in which I was blessed to make disciples of students were only a blip, considering eternity. My job was just to introduce them to Jesus and let the Spirit take care of the rest. Over time, God has shown me that making disciples and mentoring Christians isn't about me presenting my life as a "holy goal," hoping that people look at me or my teaching and become godlier. Instead, my goal is to point to Jesus in every Bible study, text, conversation, and prayer because I know that we progressively become like what we behold, and the goal is for them to be more like Jesus, not me. Jesus said, "And I, when I am lifted up from the earth, will draw all people to myself" for a good reason (John 12:32).

During the summer of 2020, I got a surprising phone call. It was from one of my former students who'd been in my Bible study five years previously. She asked if I could lead a virtual Bible study for her and about eight other women from her graduating class with whom she'd stayed in touch. She said their spiritual health was a prevalent topic in their group chat, and that they regularly lamented how much they'd taken for granted the "ready-made" Christian campus community and Bible study they'd had as undergrads.

She said, "We should have listened to you when you told us to find a good church after graduation! Yolanda, please take us back!" I just smiled as I listened to her and thought to myself "Wow! The Holy Spirit is so relentless. God is so faithful." I agreed to a four-week study of a Pauline epistle of their choosing, but I challenged them to find a healthy, local Christian community and to share what they'd learned with that community after we were done. As we partner with God in the work that he does in people, we must remember that the progressive transformation the Holy Spirit works takes time. Some of the women in that impromptu summer Bible study were women I had spent many nights crying over and praying for. Meanwhile, God was working in them the entire time.

The funny thing is, we understand the patience of God in sanctification when it comes to our lives, but we don't always apply this to discipling others. We love saying "God is working on me!" when describing our spiritual journey but wonder why God won't "hurry up with the sanctification" in someone else's life. As building blocks of the temple of the Holy Spirit, we're called to patiently walk alongside people, speaking the truth in love (Ephesians 4:15, 25) as God sanctifies them, confident that God will finish the work he has begun (Philippians 1:6). When we try to impersonate the Holy Spirit, we stunt people's spiritual growth—and our own. We rob them of the beauty of experiencing aha moments that come while seeking God and receiving new revelation from the Spirit about God's character.

JESUS IS PATIENT

Following in Jesus' footsteps means embodying patience as the Spirit sanctifies the people we're close to. After he's resurrected, Jesus engages two grieving disciples on the road (Luke 24:13-35) and in doing so embodies Psalm 34:18, revealing a patient and personal God who sees us, hears us, and empathizes with us in our sorrow. Those two disciples lacked understanding of who Jesus was (Luke 24:27-32), and Jesus patiently guided them through the entire Hebrew Bible to help them see how those Scriptures were all about him. He talked with them all day and when it got late, they begged him not to leave. He stayed and ate dinner with them, and I imagine the disciples had lots of questions and talked all night. When Jesus finally left, they marveled at how they'd felt while he patiently engaged them, not necessarily at what he taught (Luke 24:32).

On this topic, Richard Hays writes, "We do not gain a grasp of Scripture's significance solely through lectures on the text; we come to understand the death and resurrection of Jesus as we participate in the shared life of the community, enacted in meals shared at the table."[3] Jesus "opened" up the Old Testament to them as he taught them on the road, but their eyes weren't "opened" to recognize Jesus until they ate dinner together. We're not Jesus, but we can embody his patience. There's something about being around people who act like Jesus that opens eyes of faith. The Bible describes disciples of Christ like me and you as "a kind of first fruits of all that God has created" (James 1:18). God patiently nourishes us via the Holy Spirit until we bear fruit. Imagining myself and others as seedlings in God's garden of redemption gives me an eternal perspective on sanctification and helps me to be patient.

Setting expectations for how long you can disciple someone is wise to minimize hurt feelings, but keep in mind that discipleship is a lifelong process. When I'm discipling someone, I remind myself that I'm just one person in one season of their life who is sowing a seed that, prayerfully, someone else will water down the road.

If you're reading these words and feel insufficient to disciple or mentor someone, let me be the first to agree with you. Our sufficiency is from God (2 Corinthians 3:4)! It's God who works in us "to will and to act in order to fulfill his good purpose," especially in our weakness (Philippians 2:13). Discipleship is not about making super spiritual clones. You're not the Holy Spirit. When we trust in the finished work of Christ for our salvation, God begins to fold our stories into his redemption

---

[3]Richard B. Hays, "Reading Scripture in Light of the Resurrection," in *The Art of Reading Scripture*, ed. Ellen F. Davis, Richard B. Hays (Grand Rapids, MI: Eerdmans, 2003), 231.

story like egg whites in a meringue. When we're discipling someone, we're collaborating with the triune God in the work that God is doing in that person. Now, can a person look at how God has worked in your life and be encouraged? Yes. Can they look at spiritual disciplines and rhythms that have helped you to grow and learn from those patterns? Of course.

But at the end of the day, Jesus Christ is the same yesterday and today and forever—not us. The heart of discipleship is consistently pointing people to follow our faithful and steadfast Savior, and not us or our culture. I pray that remembering this takes the pressure that we put on ourselves to be the Holy Spirit in people's lives *off*. We colabor with God (Galatians 4:19) as the Holy Spirit progressively transforms and teaches people about God's nature (1 Corinthians 2:12-13). Discipleship isn't even about finding your identity in "making disciples." We find our identity primarily as followers of Christ and are called to depend on the Holy Spirit's power alone to bear the fruit of righteousness (John 15:5, 8).

I judge people who've lived in NYC for more than ten years and still only get around by using Google maps. I judge them because I'm a Brooklyn native and a snob but also because when they use a map app to get around the city, they rob themselves of the beauty of exploring and learning the city with their feet, eyes, and ears. In the same way, when we're on "speed dial" with everyone that we disciple because we secretly enjoy flexing our exegetical muscles and answering all their Bible interpretation questions, we rob them of the beauty of exploring and getting lost in God's Word as the Holy Spirit reveals God to them. When we try to rush people's sanctification, we can do so much damage. And we rob ourselves of the privilege of "bearing their burdens" and pleading with God in prayer for their spiritual growth.

I'm writing this chapter from the apartment of a young woman I began discipling and mentoring when she was in college at Columbia University over eight years ago. When she found out I was writing this book and needed a quiet place to write, she offered up her apartment to me, no questions asked. Sometimes God is gracious enough to allow us to watch people grow in Christlikeness, and she is one of those gifts. Discipleship takes time. Be patient with yourself and others and trust the Spirit.

LISTEN WELL

MOST PEOPLE THAT I KNOW, know at least one person who has lost a loved one over the past few years. When we when meet someone who is experiencing a crisis of faith or has flat-out rejected God because of the tragic loss of a loved one, we can be tempted to respond to their pain with a three-point sermon on the sovereignty of God, instead of embodying the sympathy, compassion, and understanding that they want and need. In John's narrative of Lazarus's death (John 11), which we explored earlier, Mary comes out of her house to meet Jesus and says, "Lord, if you had been here, my brother would not have died." Mary has been a disciple of Jesus for some time, and she knows who Jesus is and what he's capable of. Like Mary, there are people we know who have been following Christ for many years but have been traumatized by the loss of a friend or family member. They may confess that they feel like God doesn't care or doesn't exist, and that they feel abandoned. When people express those feelings and ask us "Where is God?" in times of tragedy, we should be listening for the core concern beneath the question and sit with them in their grief, like Jesus did for others. In those moments, as the Spirit empowers us to embody compassion, we're reminded of our shared humanity, and we imitate Jesus.

Even though he has resurrection power over death, Jesus sits with Mary and mourns the realness of death. At Lazarus's tomb, Jesus is mourner and comforter before he is resurrector. Being realistic about the brokenness of this world when we engage people with the gospel doesn't negate being hopeful. Because of the hope we have in the gospel, we can acknowledge the brokenness and wickedness in the world and be real with people that we are discipling when they are full of sorrow. We can encourage each other to follow Jesus' example and grieve in a healthy way.

In the recent past we've endured global climate change–induced natural disasters, monthly mass shootings, skyrocketing inflation, the rise of Christian nationalism, and the loss of millions of lives due to the Covid-19 pandemic. In these times, what does it look like to provide a trauma-informed theology of discipleship that matches the weight of the trauma that many have endured? As billionaires make record profits and poverty is criminalized, how do we practically follow our Savior, who intentionally laid down his liberties to be good news to the poor? How do we encourage people to live a "laid-down life" when they barely feel alive themselves? We need a more robust theology of suffering than telling hurting people that "all things work together." When will they work together? How do they work together?

I believe that discipleship in this cultural moment means explaining that James 1:2-4 ("Consider it pure joy . . . ") doesn't mean that we excuse oppression, and that suffering and systemic oppression are two different things. We also need to teach about lament as a spiritual discipline.

Lament has been a friend to me when my tears are my food over the brokenness of humanity. It might sound counterintuitive, but lament is beautiful because even though I'm crying out to God, at times cussing at God and giving voice to my suffering, I'm still speaking to God! Once I stop talking to you, it's a wrap; our relationship is over. But glory be to God that Jesus models lament for us. Lament in the Scriptures invites us to be gut-wrenchingly honest with God about our pain.

In my discipleship class, we read a powerful section on lament in Chanequa Walker-Barnes's book *I Bring the Voices of My People* and we discuss how in the movie *The Color Purple*, Celie (the protagonist) "writes letters to God in order to voice truths that are too horrific to be expressed even in prayer."[1] The body of Christ needs to be a place where people feel safe enough to bring their lament without being told that it's a spiritual deficiency. Take time to lament. We can't really lean in to our resurrection hope until we honestly lament what's broken.

As Christians we're a people characterized by hope, and our hope is in a living Savior (Matthew 12:21), who in his incarnation was murdered by state-sanctioned violence (empire). In his life, Jesus experienced the brokenness of humanity in all its fullness but still had the courage to lament and pray (Luke 13:34). Jesus didn't just suffer for us, Jesus suffered like us. We're united with a Savior who identifies with us in our suffering and who screamed out bits of Psalm 22 in lament on the cross. We need to take a cue from Jesus and lean in to lament in this cultural moment so that hope can be birthed, and so we can follow Jesus as emotionally healthy disciples.

This is why community is so important for discipleship. Sometimes lamenting on our own is too difficult. We need community to cry with, to process our feelings with, to be

---

[1]Chanequa Walker-Barnes, *I Bring the Voices of My People: A Womanist Vision for Racial Reconciliation* (Grand Rapids, MI: Eerdmans, 2019), 168-69.

angry with, to be brutally honest with, and to pray with. Healthy discipleship looks like receiving the gift of lament as a way to voice our anger and trauma while staying in communion with God and people. Following in Jesus' footsteps means learning how to wail (Jeremiah 9:17-21).

So how does receiving communal lament as a gift help bring healing where there is numbness and despair? How do we cultivate spaces where people can be honest about their pain in an emotionally healthy way?

In the summer of 2020, in response to the murders of George Floyd and Breonna Taylor at the hands of police, our local church organized a Pray and Protest march with several other NYC churches and organizations to protest police brutality. The past eight years seemed ripped from the pages of Revelation, as almost every month I learned about some brutality inflicted on Black people by racists. It seemed like the entire world was grieving the senseless killing of Black people at the hands of police, and we didn't want the church to be found missing. I was unable to attend the march, but the leader of our church's "Amos" social justice ministry asked me to write a lament liturgy to be recited aloud in a local park at the end of the march. At first, I didn't know what to write, but the Spirit led me to Psalms 9 and 10. Here's what I wrote:

Leader:
The Lord is a stronghold for the oppressed,
    a stronghold in times of trouble.

And those who know your name put their trust in you,
    for you, O Lord, have not forsaken those who seek you.

Response:
Lord, you have been our refuge,
    and you will not forsake your people.

You hear the cry of the afflicted,
and you are near to the crushed in Spirit.

Leader:

Arise, O Lord; O God, lift up your hand;
forget not the afflicted. Why does the wicked
renounce God
and say in his heart, "You will not call to account"?

But you do see, for you note mischief and vexation,
that you may take it into your hands.

To you the helpless commits himself;
you have been the helper of the fatherless.

Response:

Lord, hear our cry.

Throughout his earthly ministry, Jesus applied himself to the core human concerns of abandonment, loneliness, and doubt, and gave us himself. As his followers, we should seek to embody the compassion of Christ through the ministry of presence. After that march, I met so many people who had attended the protest and wanted to learn more about the church. Some even joined my discipleship class the following year and sought to be mentored. Another way to introduce people to the compassion of Christ is through "no-strings" benevolence and generosity. In the wake of the mass layoffs in 2020 and 2021 due to the Covid-19 pandemic, our local church created a public hardship fund as an expression of the love and compassion of Jesus by providing financial assistance to people who were struggling to survive.

In John 11, Jesus leans into his humanity and sits with his friend Mary in her sorrow. With his ministry of presence, Jesus reveals that God is a God of compassion. Let us strive to do the same. Mary wants answers and Jesus gives her his presence. Jesus had just come from the Hanukkah festival in Jerusalem, where people tried to kill him because of his messianic claims, but Jesus doesn't choose to justify himself. Instead, he prioritizes patiently listening to Mary's frustration about his absence, walks with her to see Lazarus, and then weeps with her. And in this moment, in his humanity, Jesus embodies the love of God. The kingdom of God isn't a government or a corporation—it's family. When we see Jesus as the source of our love, we can make disciples, and our communities can speak a word about what it means to be people called to continue the mission of Jesus and about who is welcome in the kingdom of God. John 11:5 tells us that Jesus loved Mary, Martha, and Lazarus. Love should be what compels us as we seek to make disciples of Christ because embodied love is what builds the body of Christ. In Hosea 14:4-8, the prophet describes the restored people of God as a fruitful and fragrant tree, planted by God, that provides shade and refuge for people. This is exactly how Jesus describes the kingdom of God in Mark 4:31-32. As we answer Jesus' discipleship call, we help populate and cultivate communities that can be refuge and shade for people who are longing to experience beauty.

LISTENING FOR THE VOICE OF JESUS

A question I often get asked is, How can I hear from God? How do I differentiate between the voices in my head and the voice of God? After his resurrection, Jesus appears to his disciple Mary at the tomb where he was buried (John 20:15-18). Jesus speaks to Mary, but she doesn't recognize him. Sometimes trauma and grief can make it hard to recognize the voice of God. Mary was one of the few disciples who witnessed Jesus' crucifixion (Mark 15:40-41), and when Jesus speaks to her at the tomb, she's still in shock and is weeping. But Jesus meets Mary in her trauma and continues to speak: "Jesus said to her, 'Mary.' She turned toward him and cried out in Aramaic, 'Rabboni!' (which means 'Teacher')" (John 20:16).

This fulfilled what Jesus described earlier in the Gospel of John: "The shepherd calls his sheep by name, and they follow because they know his voice" (John 10:3-4). When Jesus calls his sheep Mary by her name, she recognizes his voice and addresses him as a disciple. When Mary hears Jesus call her name, she knows that she is known by Jesus. When Jesus calls her name, she is reminded that she is loved by Jesus. When Jesus calls her name, she is reminded that the story of her new life in Christ is not over. She is reminded and reassured that she is more than Mary "from whom seven demons had come out" (Luke 8:2). She is reminded that she's part of a story that includes her but is bigger than she is. She knows and she is known. She sees and she is seen. She hears and she is heard.

Jesus makes sure she knows that she is seen and known and loved by him before he asks her to proclaim his resurrection to the other disciples. Just as Jesus being commissioned by his Father at his baptism was a clue that he was continuing the story of Israel, Jesus' audible commissioning of Mary is a clue that she will continue the redemptive mission of Jesus. She is loved by Jesus, just as Jesus is loved by the Father. "I am the good shepherd; I know my sheep and my sheep know me—just as the Father knows me and I know the Father" (John 10:14-15). As Mary listens to Jesus, she recognizes that she is loved and known by God and is prepared to follow in his footsteps.

Many of us try to do the work of God to gain affirmation from God that we're good Christians. But we can only follow in Jesus' footsteps and make disciples as we're reminded and reassured that we are God's new creation. This means taking time to slow down and listen to what God has already revealed to us in his Word and to what God wants to reveal to us as we pray and worship. Jesus has already spoken. He's said, "Make disciples." He's said, "I will be with you until the end of the age." He's said, "A new command I give you: Love one another. As I have loved you, so you must love one another" (John 13:34). The Bible testifies that there are secret things that belong to the Lord (Deuteronomy 29:29), but God calls us to trust him and continue his mission led by what he has spoken and by his Spirit. The question I ask myself when I'm tempted to feel a way about a perceived silence from God is, What are you doing to live out what God has already told you?

The details of how we embody these commands will look different from one person to the next because we're all unique. But let's start with what God has already spoken and live it out. This doesn't have to take place on Sunday morning. Jesus met Mary at a tomb, not in the synagogue. Hearing from God with ears of faith means asking God to speak in faith, and then taking time to listen for God's voice as we go from day to day. Let's listen well and follow.

ACKNOWLEDGMENTS

I NEVER WANTED TO WRITE A BOOK. But I'm so grateful to God for using my family and friends to help me birth a book that I wish I could've read over sixteen years ago when I started seminary.

To my dearest Rodney. Thank you for praying over me, listening, reading drafts, putting the kids to bed, and then making them breakfast in the mornings while I wrote. You encouraged me to keep writing when I wanted to give up and give the check back. I couldn't do so much of what I do without you. I love you, baby! To Samuel and Emmanuel, may you see a glimpse of the limitless love of Jesus in me and Daddy and be drawn to experience that love for yourselves. To my parents, Carol and Desmond Atkins, thank you for raising me to love Jesus and my Blackness.

To my Mt. Lebanon Baptist Church family, I am what I am because of you. To Rev. Carl A. Darrisaw, a true servant of God, you poured out your life and in doing so introduced me and so many children to Jesus. To Rev. Alvin C. Bernstine, you asked me to teach Sunday school and affirmed gifts that I didn't yet know I had. To my childhood Sunday school teachers and Girl Scout leaders, thank you. Y'all introduced me to Jesus with your lives. To all the children (who are now grown up) from the P.H.A.T.T. Friday youth group, thank you for helping to form Jesus in me. To my Rahab group ladies, thank you for showing me Jesus and for being a safe place for me and so many women. Elder Valerie Lee, thank you for saying yes and leading us.

To my City Church family and Trinity Grace Crown Heights Church family, thank you for loving me and walking with me and my family.

To my City Seminary of New York family. Maria, Mark, Vivian, Sung, Janice, Jonathan, Adebisi, Olivia, Adrienne, Gloria, Donald, Ben, Sonja, Peter, and Miriam, thank you for stretching my theological imagination and teaching me to wrestle with God's Word in community.

To Jim Black, thank you for introducing me to an amazing community of young adults at Columbia University and Barnard College that changed the course of my life. To all the students I had the pleasure to know at Columbia Faith & Action, thank you for allowing me into your lives to serve you. To my fellow Christian Union ministry fellows, I learned so much from you. Thank you! To Sara Mead, you heard I needed a quiet place to write and gave me the keys to your apartment for a week. This book doesn't get written without that week. Thank you for your generous heart. To Ava Ligh, my sister from another mother. My partner in the gospel. Thank you for your friendship and love. You've taught me so much about ministry. I'm still mad you wouldn't write this book with me, but I can't wait to read yours one day. Love you!

To Ekemini Uwan, I didn't take writing this book seriously until after recording the Truth's Table podcast interview with you and Christina. Thank you for calling me later that year convincing me that God could use me to write a book, praying for me, and showing what a book proposal was. Thank you for vouching for me and introducing me to Cindy and IVP. Thank you for lending your words to this project and writing my foreword. If "love is an action" were a person, it's you, sis! Love you!

To Eddie Harmon, Dr. Chris Burton, Dr. Maria Liu Wong, and Dr. Rachel M. B. Atkins, thank you for reading my first manuscript draft (right before Christmas) and for your thoughtful recommendations. Chanel Dokun, thank you for generously offering me your hard-won advice throughout this writing journey. Jeanelle Drysdale-Miller, thank you for being my Zoom writing accountability partner. Your prayer and presence spurred me on every week, and I'm grateful to God for you.

Special thanks to my editors at InterVarsity Press, Cindy Bunch and Nilwona Nowlin. Y'all are magicians! You took my words and crafted them into a whole book. I'm so grateful to God for your encouragement, coaching, and wisdom along this journey.

To all the donors who've supported my discipleship ministry at Epiphany Church Brooklyn since 2021, I'm grateful to God for your prayers and financial generosity in the middle of a recession and a whole pandemic. Thank you for embodying Jesus and for your partnership in the gospel.

Finally, to Epiphany Church Brooklyn, Pastor Brandon Watts, Pastor Timi Ogunfowora, and Ty Watts. Thank you for supporting this project before I had the courage to write it. Thank you for trusting me to teach the Bible and make disciples at Epiphany Church. Thank you for including childcare for Rodney and me in the church budget so that I could take time off to write. To the Epiphany Church staff, Gabe, Ed, Valerie, and Chelsea, it's a blessing to serve with y'all. To all my Epiphany Church fam and every God Seekers Discipleship Class graduate, thank you for allowing me to serve you. To God be the glory!

PRAYER AND THE HOLY SPIRIT

SAMPLE TRUTH TO PRAXIS ACTIVITY 1

THE GOAL OF THIS EXERCISE is to help us become more aware of the role of the Holy Spirit in our prayer lives. You can ask the following questions to get a sense of your mentee's relationship to prayer:

- What are some personal obstacles to prayer for you?

- While you're praying, what makes prayer difficult?

Take time this week to do this exercise: Sit in stillness and silence for five minutes, and then read through a psalm of praise. (Examples: Psalm 30, 100, or 136.) Write down whatever comes to mind as you reflect on the psalm and offer up a prayer of response to God.

Read through Acts 16:16-40 and answer the questions below:

- How can God use prayer to encourage us and those we pray with?

- Reflecting on Paul and Silas's response to the jailer, how can prayer prepare and transform us to be agents of grace to those around us?

Note for discipleship leader: Paul and Silas were in prison. They've been beaten and are suffering for preaching the gospel (1 Thessalonians 2:2). But around midnight, they begin to worship and pray. Their captors and fellow captives were listening to them sing and pray (corporate worship is powerful). They obviously noticed that Paul and Silas were different. The same Spirit that led them to Phillipi and empowered them to preach the gospel also empowered them to pray during their suffering and captivity. There's a miraculous earthquake, and Paul and Silas are freed, but more importantly everyone in the prison is transformed by worship and prayer. The worship and prayer while they were suffering prepared Paul and Silas to be agents of life, peace, and reconciliation to the jailer and his family. What led the jailer to believe? He saw the continuation of the ministry and power of Jesus in Paul and Silas.

Read through Luke 12:11-12 and Psalm 42:8 together aloud. Reflect on how prayer is a Spirit-led act of colaboring with God.

Read through 2 Corinthians 10:4 and Ephesians 6:10-18 together. Discuss whether or not you're prone to pray in response to evil and suffering. Do you believe that spiritual warfare is real? Why or why not? Do you believe that prayer is a viable weapon of spiritual warfare?

Read through Acts 2–4 and answer the questions below:

- How do the corporate prayers of Peter, John, and the community of disciples in Acts 4:23-31 reveal how they are following in Jesus' footsteps?

- How does the Holy Spirit empower Peter's discipleship ministry? Compare Peter's words and actions in Acts 2–4 to his words and actions in Luke 22:24-61.

- In Acts 4:23-31, what attributes of God do Peter, John, and the community of disciples meditate on while they pray?

How can meditating on these attributes while you pray encourage you?

- Read Numbers 11:29 and then reread Acts 4:23-36. How does the Holy Spirit work in the prayer life and the common life of the community of disciples to transform them? Read Ephesians 2:18-22. How can the Spirit do the same for us?

PSALM 19 BIBLE INTERPRETATION EXERCISE

SAMPLE TRUTH TO PRAXIS ACTIVITY 2

THIS EXERCISE WILL HELP US examine our relationship to God's Word.

Print out a copy of Psalm 19. Read Psalm 19 twice, then make an outline of the psalm. An outline is a basic summary of a Scripture passage. Look for main points and subplots. When making an outline ask yourself, how would I summarize the sections of Psalm 19 in my own words? What is the psalmist trying to say? Here's a sample outline:

Psalm 19:1-6: Personification of creation declaring God's glory

Psalm 19:7-9: Description of the various qualities of laws, commands of God

Psalm 19:10-11: Rewards of obeying God's commands

Psalm 19:12-14: The psalmist is asking God to help him keep the law so he can also bring God glory through his words (spoken and unspoken)

Say: Repetition is a poetic device to reinforce a thought. Let's read through the psalm again. This time let's look for and underline repeated words, phrases, and ideas to get clues about the central concern of the psalm. What is repeated in this psalm? What emotion does the repetition of these words evoke in the psalmist? Go back and look at your outline. How is this psalm structured? How does this psalm move from beginning to end?

Application questions (Don't rush here!):

- What does this passage reveal to you about God's character?

- How does this revelation about God's character affect how you see yourself?

Notes for discipleship leader: God wants to reveal who he is through his Word and God intends to form us through that revelation. This is a psalm about the character of God's Word. It's a poem about the power of the revelation of the creative and transformative Word of God.

PSALM 19:1-6

Movement: The psalmist starts out describing how God's voice speaks through non-human creation to everyone human. The psalmist then describes how God's Word transforms God's covenant people, Israel. Finally, he asks God to transform him in such a way that would make his words (his voice) acceptable in the sight of God.

Structure: There is lots of parallelism in this psalm. There is metaphor and personification. Verses 1-4 all have key words and phrases that have to do with speaking: "declare," "proclaim," "pour forth speech," "reveal," and "their voice goes out."

Ask: What does the repetition of these declarative words reveal? Why are they there?

The repetitive use of these declarative terms and the metaphor of the non-verbal speech of creation reinforces how God's creation "speaks" a universal language that glorifies God—just by existing.

PSALM 19:7-10

Ask: In verses 7-10, what's the purpose of the Word? What does the Word reveal?

Ask: What does the repetitive nature of the description of God's Word reveal about how the psalmist feels about it? How does this psalm make you feel about God's Word?

Using six synonyms to describe God's law, the psalmist describes how God's attributes are displayed through God's Word, thus glorifying God and opening the eyes of God's people so they might see him more clearly. God's Word reveals and God's Word transforms. "YHWH" is the personal name of Israel's covenant God in the Old Testament. "Using adjectives and participle phrases, the psalmist describes the excellence of YHWH's revelation."[1] YHWH's Word is "perfect," "sure," "right," "pure," "clean," "true" and "righteous altogether"—just like YHWH. "So described, [the] law almost becomes the immediate presence of Yahweh with Israel"[2] The synonymous, repetitive parallelism of the psalmist expresses the delight of the psalmist in YHWH's Word. The mood of this portion of the poem is celebratory and full of gratitude.

Ask: Where is Psalm 19 in the metanarrative of Scripture?

---

[1]Kyle M. Yates, "The Psalms," in *The Wycliffe Bible Commentary: Old Testament*, ed. Charles F. Pfeiffer (Chicago: Moody Press, 1990), 502.

[2]Carroll Stuhlmueller, "Psalms," in *The HarperCollins Bible Commentary*, ed. James L. Mays, with the Society of Biblical Literature (San Francisco: HarperSanFrancisco, 2000), 402.

Jewish literature asserted that Jews (as descendants of Abraham) were chosen by God and were under a covenant that enabled them to keep the law. They believed that the law as a covenant system gave and supported life (Leviticus 18:5, Ezekiel 20) and was able to be kept by the grace of God (Deuteronomy 30:11-14). However, the Old Testament documents the disobedience of Israel before, during, and after the exile (and subsequent judgment of YHWH) in Assyria and Babylon.

PSALM 19:11-14

At this point in the psalm, the psalmist turns inward. After exulting in God's law, beholding God's attributes, and being moved into God's presence, God's Word begins to pierce his heart and convict him of his sin. He recognizes the power of God's Word to make clear the danger of sin and the blessings of obedience. The psalmist shows spiritual maturity in verses 12-13 by recognizing his sin and begging YHWH to "keep him from hidden faults" and "presumptuous sins" and keep them from "ruling over him." He recognizes that "head knowledge" of the law will not keep him from sin that he willfully commits (Numbers 15:30-31) and that only God can keep humanity from sinning against God (Genesis 20:6, Galatians 2:16).

Finally, the psalmist ends his "wisdom-hymn" with a prayer for redemption that encapsulates the three sections of the psalm. The psalmist longs for his words and even his inner thoughts to declare the glory of God like the heavens do. But in order for this to happen, the psalmist petitions God to personally redeem his heart and purify his words, to do for him what he in his own strength cannot do. In the midst of an uncertain world, the psalmist knows that if YHWH does these things, his "sacrifices of praise" will be accepted by YHWH (Hebrews 13:15).

The New Testament teaches that God's final revelatory event takes place in the person of Jesus (Hebrews 1:1-2) who fulfills the law that the psalmist describes. Jesus, not just his words but Jesus himself (his entire life, death, and resurrection), is how God reveals himself to humanity. Second Timothy 3:14-16 teaches that the "Holy Scriptures" (the Old Testament) lead somewhere—that is, they are not an end in themselves. The Holy Scriptures (the Old Testament) lead us to wisdom (Christ), who brings salvation through faith in him (1 Corinthians 1:30). Luke Timothy Johnson put it this way: "The scripture illuminates the story of Jesus in his faithful gift of himself for humans and his story provides the telos (end, goal) for scripture itself."[3]

Read John 1:1-3, 14 and then ask yourself these questions:

- How is Jesus embedded in Psalm 19?

- How is the poetry of Psalm 19 embodied in Christ?

CHRISTOLOGICAL OUTLINE OF PSALM 19

Psalm 19:1-6. Jesus declares the glory of God because creation was created by Christ (John 1:3). Jesus is the glory of God made flesh (Hebrews 1:3: he's "the radiance of God's glory"). Jesus is the living Word of God who reveals the glory, love, and grace of God.

Psalm 19:7-10. Jesus is the fulfillment of the law (Matthew 5:17; Romans 10:4).

Psalm 19:11-14. In love, Jesus rescues sinners from the power and penalty of sin so that sin will not rule over and enslave us. Because Jesus offered himself as a living sacrifice to atone for our sins, we can offer ourselves as a living sacrifice, holy and acceptable to God, without any fear.

---

[3]Luke Timothy Johnson, *The First and Second Letters to Timothy: A New Translation with Introduction and Commentary* (New York: Doubleday, 2001), 424.

SONG OF SALVATION

"Let the message of Christ dwell among you richly as you teach and admonish one another with all wisdom through psalms, hymns, and songs from the Spirit, singing to God with gratitude in your hearts."

COLOSSIANS 3:16

"Be filled with the Spirit, speaking to one another with psalms, hymns, and songs from the Spirit. Sing and make music from your heart to the Lord, always giving thanks to God the Father for everything, in the name of our Lord Jesus Christ."

EPHESIANS 5:18-19

WHEN YOU COMPARE Colossians 3:16 with Ephesians 5:18-19, it's clear that the fruit of being filled with the Spirit and the effects of Jesus' words working in our hearts are very similar—namely, a community where disciples edify and teach each other by singing "songs from the Spirit" with thanksgiving. Jesus describes this as being sanctified by the truth (John 17:17);

the prophet Jeremiah described it as having the law being written on our hearts (Jeremiah 31:33); Isaiah described it by saying, "Your ears will hear a voice behind you, saying, 'This is the way; walk in it'" (Isaiah 30:21); I describe it as the Holy Spirit.

I like to think of the gospel of Jesus Christ as a "Spirit song" that God places in our hearts by the power of the Holy Spirit (1 Corinthians 2:9-13) to remind us of God's covenant commitment to save those who've trusted in him for salvation (Romans 1:17). As we read the Gospel narratives and our hearts are transformed by the truth, beauty, and goodness that Jesus embodies in his life, we begin to believe that another world is possible. We are empowered to follow Jesus as the Spirit of Christ whispers, *This is true, sis* and *This is possible for you, brother* to our souls.

Discipleship and mentoring relationships are beautiful when they're a relational context for people who share in the same Holy Ghost buffet to sing "spirit songs" that sustain and fuel our joy in this broken world. As I think about discipleship, I ask myself, What do these songs sound like, and what are the lyrics? Jesus promised his disciples that he would send the Spirit to guide us into wisdom and truth (John 16:13, 15:26). There's a connection between listening for the guidance of the Holy Spirit and discerning how to encourage people that we're discipling without patronizing them or minimizing their pain.

However, the evil and suffering that is part and parcel of living in this broken world can break our hearts and cause us to forget the words to the song of our salvation. Life happens and we begin to doubt that we'll ever see the goodness of the Lord in the land of the living or that God cares about us. There have been countless times when thoughts of *Yo, is God a sham?* invade my prayer closet. In these moments I've needed someone to sit with me in the shadows, sing that song of salvation to me, and remind me (as Jesus did with Thomas) to bring my doubt to God and rest in the reality of God's faithfulness.

One of the groups of people I've had to sing "spirit songs" to are women who are victims of sexual assault. Sadly, sexual assault is so prevalent, especially among undergraduate college students, that statistically, if there were four women in my Bible study, one of them would be a sexual assault victim.[1] How do you sing a "spirit song" to a victim of sexual violence who is retraumatized every time they share their story with you or someone else? Being guided by the Spirit to sing a song of salvation sometimes looks like rebuking the lie that sanctification is about God ordaining suffering for "our good," then pointing a friend to a Savior who knows how it feels to be unjustly snatched by violent men, and praying that the Word will find a home in their hearts to bring about healing. Sometimes when my words are few, I read through John 19:23 and humbly share the wisdom of women much wiser than I am.

From Christina Edmondson:

Jesus knows what it means to have His clothes ripped from His body. Jesus knows what it means to have His naked, bruised and vulnerable body on display. Jesus knows what it means to have folks run from and ignore

---

[1]"Among undergraduate students, 26.4% of females and 6.8% of males experience rape or sexual assault through physical force, violence, or incapacitation." David Cantor et al., "Report on the AAU Campus Climate Survey on Sexual Assault and Misconduct," prepared for the Association of American Universities, January 17, 2020, www.aau.edu/sites/default/files/AAU-Files/Key-Issues/Campus-Safety/Revised%20Aggregate%20report%20%20and%20appendices%201-7_(01-16-2020_FINAL).pdf.

His suffering at the Cross. Jesus knows what it means to have people deny completely His experience.[2]

From Wil Gafney:

The Jesus of the gospels may have answered to the Son of David, but He lived like, laughed like, loved like, wept like & suffered like the son of Bathsheba.[3]

In those moments, "spirit songs" become a lifeline and key to applying gospel truth to the soul-sucking trauma caused by sexual assault and the shame that survivors experience. In those moments, Jesus deeply empathizes and identifies with every assault survivor, because on the cross he bore the iniquity of this world to bring healing where sin has caused brokenness.

Because God placed this salvation song in our hearts through the Holy Spirit, the melody is eternal, even if the pain of this life causes us to forget the lyrics. And so, when we spend time encouraging someone to remember the promises of God, and we pray with them, listen to their struggles, and cry with them, call a suicide line with them, or study the Word with them, we sing the song of their salvation. The next thing you know they'll start to remember the lyrics that they'd forgotten, and we'll all sing together. And it's music to God's ears.

Eventually they'll know that song so good, they can sing it for someone else.

Much of discipleship is the Spirit nudging my spirit with God's promises, which turns up the volume of the song of

[2]Christina Edmondson, "#Jesustoo for #Metoo" Day 17: The King Is Coming: A Truth's Table Advent Devotional, December 17, 2018, https://jude3project.org /truthstable/day172018.

[3]Wil Gafney, "Rev. Dr. Wil Gafney: What if Bathsheba Took the Throne?" McMurry University Fall Religion Lectureship, Abilene, TX, October 24, 2022, www.youtube .com/watch?v=QYmpwaw5P-Y&t=14s.

salvation in my own heart. And when I'm talking to someone else who might be struggling, I can hum the song to them. Sometimes this looks like reminding men and women that they have worth, dignity, and value apart from their résumés, waistlines, relationship statuses, and MCAT scores. Other times, it looks like reminding people who are tired of convincing fellow Christians why Black lives should matter, that darker skin is not a curse, and that God loves them, even though the United States may not. Sometimes it's a *God loves you, sis! You got your eyes on so many things, but don't forget to keep your eyes on Jesus, who is perfecting you.* But it's also reminding people of who God is by tangibly loving them. It's one thing to pray for people, and it's another thing to remind people of the promises of God by being the answer to some of their prayers.

Sometimes this looks like telling a single parent that you'll "pray their strength" and offering to babysit their children. Sometime this looks like praying for healing for a sick friend and going to the hospital or doctor with them. Sometimes this looks like praying that God provides employment for an out-of-work young man and offering to edit a poorly written résumé. The truth is, we've always needed each other this much, but the Covid-19 pandemic recently made me acutely aware of how barren life is without meaningful community. I recall a check-in phone call with a member of my church where, after I said, "Hello. How are you doing? How can I pray for you?" she burst into tears because she lived alone—which used to be a stunt before the pandemic—and was drowning under the weight of the grief of losing her mother. I lost track of time as we prayed and through tears sang a "song of the Spirit" over the phone to this dear soul. But I believe that the phone call itself was a song in and of itself that reminded her that she was not forgotten. And this goes both ways. I love when someone that I'm mentoring asks to pray for me or asks me how I'm doing because it reveals that they want to participate in the sacred work that God wants to do in my life.

And what a privilege to partner with our brothers and sisters, to encourage and to be encouraged by reminding each other of a love that we once knew but sometimes forget. What a privilege to be called as when Jesus called Lazarus's friends in Bethany, to help someone untangle and unwrap themselves from anger, despair, or depression by reminding them of God's promises, while the Holy Spirit does the heavy lifting of heart transformation. The sanctifying soul transformation that happens in discipleship is a holy collaboration. I'm regularly amazed that the triune God invites "the most problematic inhabitants of the earth"[4] to participate in it.

In his epic book *Life Together*, Dietrich Bonhoeffer writes,

> The Christian needs another Christian who speaks God's word to him. He needs him again and again when he becomes uncertain and discouraged, for by himself he cannot help himself without belying the truth. He needs his brother man as a bearer and proclaimer of the divine word of salvation. . . . The Christ in his own heart is weaker than the Christ in the word of his brother. His own heart is uncertain, his brothers is sure.[5]

Our faith toward God and our love for one another flows from Christ, the source of our living hope. If we have faith and

---

[4]Colin E. Gunton, *Christ and Creation: The Didsbury Lectures,* 1990 (Eugene, OR: Wipf and Stock Publishers, 2005), 33.
[5]Dietrich Bonhoeffer, *Life Together: The Classic Exploration of Christian Community,* trans. John W. Doberstein (New York: HarperOne, 1954), 23.

love without hope, we'll burn out. If we have faith and hope without love, we're hypocrites.[6] Only God knows what trials and tribulations are around the corner, but I know that without hope we will not endure. My hope in what God has begun in Jesus and in God's promised future fuels my faith in God and helps me love people *today*. Lord, would you fuel our hope today? Remind us of the power of new life we have through the Holy Spirit today. Remind us, Holy Ghost, that the power and penalty of sin have been defeated because of Jesus' sacrifice on the cross. Remind us to sing your Spirit song to each other and help us to love who, what, and how you love.

---

[6]Many thanks to my brother in Christ Pastor Nick Nowalk for his teaching about the triad of faith, hope, and love throughout the New Testament and how they work together.

QUESTIONS FOR REFLECTION AND DISCUSSION

1. Who have you recently sung the song of salvation to? Who is your karaoke partner in the faith?

2. What "spirit songs" do you have on repeat?

3. What promises of God are you struggling to believe?

4. Who would it be unimaginable for you to show compassion to?

CHAPTERS 1-6

1. Where has culture and tradition been infused into your idea of discipleship?

2. Below are a few Scriptures that speak to journeying with others through difficult times. Meditate on the Scriptures below and identify two or three people you can begin to practice this with.

> Confess your sins to one another and pray for one another, that you may be healed. (James 5:16)

> Let us consider how to stir up one another to love and good works, not neglecting to meet together, as

is the habit of some, but encouraging one another, and all the more as you see the Day drawing near. (Hebrews 10:24-25)

But exhort one another every day, as long as it is called "today," that none of you may be hardened by the deceitfulness of sin. (Hebrews 3:13)

Bear one another's burdens, and so fulfill the law of Christ. (Galatians 6:2)

Encourage the fainthearted, help the weak, be patient with them all. See that no one repays anyone evil for evil, but always seek to do good to one another and to everyone. Rejoice always, pray without ceasing. (1 Thessalonians 5:14-17)

3. Read Acts 2:42-47 and list the activities that these early Christians committed themselves to and practice in response to the preaching of the Christ's resurrection and the pouring out of the Spirit on the church. What activities listed here do you find most challenging or frustrating? Identify one or two people you can talk to about growing together in those areas.

4. Who can you tell the truth about Jesus to with your life? What attributes of Jesus do you most embody? Take some time to reflect and pray about this.

5. If you're a leader in your local church, think about how your church demonstrates the good news of the gospel through community life. Write down what comes to mind and pray for a few new people to join in that work.

6. Read 1 Peter 4:10 and 1 Corinthians 12 and spend some time praying for discernment about spiritual giftings. Then reach out and ask a trusted friend or two what gifts they recognize in you.

1. Where is the active and manifest presence of God for you? Where can you currently see the glory of God's goodness in your neighborhood?

2. Read through Colossians 3:12-17. How do these "clothes" fit on you? Which one of these Christlike virtues is difficult to put on? Do you extend these virtues to other people? Do you extend them to yourself? Who can help you clothe yourself with Christ?

3. Do you see rest as a blessing or a burden? How can you make some time to rest this week?

4. How are you tempted by Satan in the wilderness (difficult) seasons of life? In those times, what are you tempted to trust in?

5. Read Matthew 3–4 and Hebrews 4 and 10 and spend time answering these questions:

   • When life makes you doubt who God says you are, does Scripture help?

   • Does the Word of God help you to love people?

   • Do you primarily use the Word of God as a weapon to argue with people? With yourself? Why or why not?

   • When was the last time the Word of God caused you to love God, someone else, or yourself more deeply?

   • What's your relationship with the Word of God like? Does it sustain you?

   • How does God's Word inform your relationship with yourself?

Like this book?
Scan the code to discover more content like this!

Get on IVP's email list to receive special offers, exclusive book news, and thoughtful content from your favorite authors on topics you care about.

InterVarsity Press